UNKNOWN
PLEASURES

Also by Andy Kirkpatrick

Psychovertical
Cold Wars
1001 Climbing Tips

ANDY

COLLECTED WRITING ON LIFE, DEATH, CLIMBING AND EVERYTHING IN BETWEEN

KIRKPATRICK

UNKNOWN PLEASURES

Vertebrate Publishing, Sheffield
www.v-publishing.co.uk

*'Who can break from the
snares of the world'*

HAN-SHAN

UNKNOWN PLEASURES
ANDY KIRKPATRICK

First published in 2018 by Vertebrate Publishing.

 VERTEBRATE PUBLISHING
Crescent House, 228 Psalter Lane, Sheffield S11 8UT, United Kingdom.
www.v-publishing.co.uk

This book is a work of non-fiction based on the life of Andy Kirkpatrick.
The author has stated to the publishers that, except in such minor respects not
affecting the substantial accuracy of the work, the contents of the book are true.

A CIP catalogue record for this book is available from the British Library.

ISBN: 978-1-911342-72-4 (Hardback)
ISBN: 978-1-911342-73-1 (Paperback)
ISBN: 978-1-911342-88-5 (Ebook)

10 9 8 7 6 5 4 3 2 1

Design and production by Jane Beagley.
www.v-publishing.co.uk

Vertebrate Publishing is committed to printing on paper from sustainable sources.

Printed and bound in the UK by T.J. International Ltd, Padstow, Cornwall.

CONTENTS

PREFACE

When the singer Freddie Mercury was dying of Aids he told those in charge of his legacy to do what they wanted with his music, his only wish being 'don't make me boring'.

Unknown Pleasures is a collection of writing covering a broad range of subjects, from Antarctic expeditions to Steven Seagal, and big-wall solos to suicide. Covering life and death and all the stuff in between, this is much more than a straight climbing book. Within these pages are stories that will terrify, stories that will make you chuckle, and stories that will make you confused, angry or even make you cry. Within this book there will be words to love and words to hate, but I promise you, none of them will be boring.

INTRODUCTION

I sit in Las Vegas, the air conditioning making me shiver, typing away –
backwards and forwards, type and delete – trying to write an introduction
that I might actually take the time to read for a book of my words.

It seems funny to have such a book, with my words printed inside it, and
it's with no false modesty that I say I don't really see myself as a writer – this
writing stuff nothing to do with me. If I was to come up with a reason for
this embarrassment of inadequacy it would be that writing has always been
such a struggle, from the moment I started school, to now as I sit and shiver.
There's no way I can claim such a title as 'writer'. To find something so
difficult robs you of any feeling of mastery, mastery being a requirement for
such a book as this, my 'greatest hits'. And so instead of being a writer I see
myself as being something else: part thief and part connector of discordant
events, mining the past. Oh and last lines, I'm good at last lines.

First to the thievery.

The words in this book were most often not really freely given but taken,
sometimes stolen against the wills of the characters described, from people
who had no clue that my writer's brain was casing away everything said and
done and experienced. The more you can steal the better; the stuff people
want left out is more often than not the only stuff to put in.

Having gone through so much past writing looking for the good stuff for
this book, I would also add myself to the list of injured parties, my own life
picked through for nuggets that could be forged into something of value to
the reader – no thought to the crime in it. All that mattered was the words,
even ones that did me harm.

There is also some criminal boldness needed to write stories that people
want to read: a little raw, a bit edgy, car-crash uncomfortable – things that
make people read through their fingers, things they've not quite read before,
things they want to read but didn't know it. I'm often asked if those who

I've written about are still alive (yes, they are), or if others mind so honest a sharing (often not), or if I share too much (yes, I do). All that really matters is that the words are read, criminal or not. As I've said, I'm not a writer of skill, but a thief – have been so long before the words – and that urge to read what I write is often just the thrill of being in on the job.

As for connections, this really seems to be what I'm good at and has very little to do with the art of writing, of planning and structure and knowing your beginning, middle and end. I was once diagnosed as being extremely dyslexic, regarded as a problem at the time – an excuse. But I soon saw it as a gift, allowing me to deconstruct and rebuild complex things, a story nothing but a pattern of words and meanings that can be pulled apart. These stories I tell are very often confused and complex, going here and there, which some wrongly assume to be designed that way, that in the madness there is deeper meaning and intellect. There is not, I just start writing and see where my easily distracted brain takes me – oh look, a squirrel – but you're welcome to extract a higher meaning if you wish. This distraction is also tied to my adventurous spirit, in that I don't want certainty, to know what comes next, what lies around every corner, only the certainty that the next paragraph has the potential to be different to this one and unexpected.

Once upon a time and long enough ago to share and not face prosecution, I was more than a word thief.

My thievery did not involve diamonds, bars of gold, or fancy sports cars, but cheese. Maybe you can go to prison for such a crime, or be sent to hell, but in my defence, this was the cheapest of cheese m'lud, not the good stuff that stinks out your house. It was hardly cheese at all, more soft orange rubber, showing that at least back then I felt some shame. The wrapper of this ill-gotten gain was labelled *Happy Shopper, Cheddar, strong*, strong cheese the only one worth the risk of being caught for – after all, life is too short for mild.

Happy Shopper was a popular brand back then in the 1990s, each item like a little Red Cross parcel to the cash-strapped: single mums, men who lived alone, the elderly, the downtrodden, people spread as thin as can be on their small slice of life. And so such offerings were true to their word, bringing happiness to shoppers with an affordable bounty of cheap cuts and slices and measures, sold in corner shops and Asian supermarkets everywhere.

Back in those days my income was about twenty-four pounds a week – I was spread thin enough to be transparent, on the dole like almost everyone else my age. It was a substance I had to stand in line once a fortnight to receive, stand in line and recite my National Insurance number and then 'sign on'.

Standing in line has a calming effect on animals, like cattle and human beings, some order to the chaotic scramble that is a life, the line that must hold for the sake of civilisation, but often without considering its possible abattoir end. When we humans stand in line we stand in line to demonstrate for fairness, in the belief that although slow you will be in some way rewarded for your patience and civic conformity, as well as the solidarity of the tut and grumble at those that push in, or who don't wait their turn (Italians).

Everyone who worked for the DHSS[1], the 'SS', where I stood in line waiting to sign on, looked like a teacher: stern, detached, disinterested, just clocking their days away, sheepdogs to us queuing sheep. '*Next*' as good as a bark, the security guard standing ready to nip the unruly. The best thing about them looking like teachers was they created a seamless join between school and unemployment – made you realise you were as loved by the state as a paper clip. I guess it was around this time, facing the back of some fellow unfortunate, that the words in this book began to form, like a grain of sand within an oyster, some small thought that there must be more to life than this – even if it was via the one thing I knew for certain I was crap at.

Once signed on, and with no bank account, your giro would be taken to the post office, and another line. The money counted out by someone else who looked like a teacher, no chit-chat or '*how are things?*', even though there was no shame in it really, that money given, like medicine, the hope being to keep the patient alive until the world got better. At the post office counter the money would be doled out, meant to last until the lines beckoned again.

Money was put aside for gas, electricity, water and food, and small loans of a pound or two paid back. Rent was taken care of by the fact that no one in the house paid rent, the owner of the flat seemingly disappeared. Drink and drugs would have been a nice distraction in those days, but not on such a tight budget, drugs only really affordable if you started dealing, any profit to be had squandered in a hazy and wasteful distraction. The only real frivolity was going out, pound-shop clubs, where dancing was free and other people's dregs could easily be drunk. On tiny dance floors with low ceilings, to the beat of Iggy Pop or the Stone Roses, you forgot just who or what you were. Bodies brushed over crunching glass, the drumming moment your own little movie as the strobe bulb pulsed through the choking smoke machine. Life was good in the dark – until the lights came on and you realised where you were, other people's sweat dripping down

---

1 Department of Health and Social Security.

on you from the ceiling. Again, that small piece of sand spun deep within, the urge to somehow make a reality which worked *with* the lights on.

In this underclass of youth poverty – although we did not see it that way, more that we were equal – there also swam the student, who although looking poor and speaking poor always seemed to have money, education and the state's largesse. They lived on loans, cheap credit and cash from home – always money for drink and drugs and patty and chips or pizza on the way home. I was so ignorant then that I was bedazzled by these students, these sophisticates far from here, unlike anyone I knew, doing degrees in English literature, politics or physics, even though all they ever seemed to do was sleep and drink. And yet I understood they had keys I did not possess, knew so much more about the world and things unknown by me – about real culture, movies, music, history and philosophy. Someone once spoke for twenty minutes about *Gulliver's Travels*, how it was a satire on society and state and religion, the inherent corruption of me and how we could be corrupted, which was news to me, as I thought it was a kids' book. It made me wonder what else I was missing. To sit in front rooms with such people was to hot-wire my empty brain to theirs for a little while, a parasite to the current that seemed to flow between them all, not just drink and drugs but also knowledge. Books, films, bands: *The Wasp Factory, Taxi Driver*, Bongwater. Drop by drop I sucked it up, filled myself in, overwrote my ignorance, an education I had missed. Most of all I could see that these people were only passing through, but also that some around me were not, that thirty years later they would still be signing on. These students though, unlike me, would one day be leaving this place, and not by the abattoir.

Back to the cheese.

A block of cheese cost about a pound in the 1990s and so was a luxury I could not afford. We lived on cheap Happy Shopper white bread (if we were flush) and twenty-five kilos of potatoes, which is a lot of potatoes: fried, boiled, mashed and baked. I don't remember ever eating any other vegetable in this time and it's surprising we never got scurvy, but we did have ketchup, so maybe there's my answer. Added to this minimalist diet was a huge tub of margarine so big it could hardly fit in the fridge and of a quality so low it could grease machinery. Such a diet was not conducive to good health but it sufficed, the cost of each meal – which was once a day – giving that warm glow whereby you know you'll not starve tomorrow or next week.

Then one day, shopping in the Asian supermarket for milk, one luxury we had to afford as tea was another staple, I looked down at the eggs and cheese and was taken over by some impulse. I couldn't stand it any more;

I had to have cheese. Cheap, oily, chemically coloured and flavoured, but cheese nonetheless. The cost of such a luxury was beyond me, and then a voice in my head just said '*steal it*' – a hot and terrible excitement coming over me. No one was looking. What did I have to lose? And so just like that, like some Artful Dodger, I reached down, past the Edam and Boursin, to the Happy Shopper Cheddar and slipped the cheapest of cheese into my pocket.

This petty thievery was long ago, the shop I stole from long gone, as is that semi-poverty that spurred the desire to rob, a poverty not really measured in pounds and pence – as I've been just as poor or worse since – but some poverty of hope and expectation that gave me just enough hunger for something better than that to set me free, gifted me that grain of sand, this book perhaps its pearl. Stealing cheese is wrong, but it was also necessary, and nothing to do with food – although I remember how great it tasted on a baked potato drenched in axle grease – more an act of stepping from the line.

And now for the end, the last line.

A few nights after my thievery, and in a cheesy glow, I called around to a house I did not really know, meeting up with some students before heading to a club. I knocked on the door and a cool Scottish student called Ewen let me in. While people sat drinking cider in the living room, watching *Married with Children* on VHS, we went up to Ewen's bedroom to wait. Unknown to us then we would become good friends, escape to London together, work in the same shop, him with his degree, me without, sit on the Tube side by side, live in the same house – but back then we were strangers. I had the eye of a burglar in such situations and made an inventory of his room: white racing bike leant against the radiator, rows of vinyl laid in line before an expensive-looking record player, a large empty backpack slipped in between the wardrobe and the wall. I asked Ewen about it, if he went walking or climbing, that part of me just a spark, and he told me about going to India. I asked him if they had McDonald's in India. They did. Then I looked beyond his treasures, to the strange and mysterious posters around his room, not Jim Morrison or The Beatles or Klimt like all the rest, but Hüsker Dü, Felt and Daniel Johnston. My heart ached to be so cool. This was no ordinary student I thought, but a man of taste and refinement, better than the others, a man to study closely and follow, a star on which to try and hitch.

I noticed a poster I'd missed in the dim room, one darker than the rest, stuck above his stereo and almost camouflaged against the dark wallpaper. It was the coolest poster I had ever seen. It was black, and created by the graphic designer Peter Saville, although I didn't know him, or what graphic design was, back then. The poster was dark and so sparse and minimalist, just layers of radio waves from pulsar CP 1919, but looking to me like overlaid cardiographs or a deep-sea survey. It was powerful. I stared at it, feeling it had some deeper, more profound meaning for me, some hidden message within those lines, the only words printed top and bottom, the only clue that this was no abstract art, but just another music poster. The name of the band, printed at the top, was Joy Division, its singer by then already dead, hanging himself in his living room on the eve of success. The words at the bottom, the album's title, an album I'd yet to hear but one that would not disappoint when soon I did: *Unknown Pleasures*.

Andy Kirkpatrick
Las Vegas, November 2017

ILLUSTRATIONS

The moment I could hold a crayon in my hand I began to make marks. I sat in my high chair, scribbling away, my art both a mess and a start. I loved to draw and so I drew a lot, every spare moment when I wasn't playing or being schooled, spent laid on my stomach in front of the TV drawing.

While many kids would be fantasising about having an Atari, I was daydreaming about paper. My uncle Clive was a printer and so gave me huge stacks of card to draw on, funny offcuts for my scribblings which were piled up in the sideboard, drawn down a centimetre a day. These offcuts were never even, they could not be folded top to bottom, side to side, the edges matched and perfect, like A papers can, but awkwardly, overlapping, the cuts made imperfectly and so not matching. I dreamt of Daler Rowney pads, especially their monster A1 one, thinking perhaps on paper so squared away I'd be straight myself, easily folded and folded again, edges always matching. But those offcuts were a great match for my stupid brain, which could decode the comic pictures but not the comic words. So that's what I drew, stories formed from pictures in tiny imperfect squares. For me, real words were born within speech bubbles. Lying on a beanbag in front of *Grange Hill*, I thought I was making pictures, but really this was the only way I knew how to tell stories.

When you do something a lot you become good at it, and being good at drawing when you're at school earns you as much kudos as being able to kick a ball or get the girls. That skill is one that's always in demand. Then one day, while drawing a Harrier jet fighter in a science class for some other kid, I had a sudden revelation: being good a drawing is not about the marks you make with your pencil, but a result of taking the time to see, to look, to notice. The reason I could draw a great fighter plane had nothing to do with that classic 'eye' – to draw a line – but the fact that I cared to notice where that line would be, that there were panels and vanes there, that bombs hung from the fuselage as well as from the wings, that through the glass you could see the ejector seat handles, striped yellow and black. What makes an artist is not what they draw, it's that they see the vital importance of the seemingly unimportant.

That was a very long time ago, but that little thought – in my ten-year-old head – has always stuck with me, reminded me to keep looking, to take the time, long after I put down those childish pencils, and it's perhaps led from one set of marks to another – what you find in these pages.

CLIMBING, EXPEDITIONS AND ADVENTURES

1.1

THE LAND OF GREEN GINGER

One night when I was sixteen we found a battered car and escaped from the city. We drove north to the coast, to a secret place few of us believed existed; maybe myth, just bait to the imagination, but maybe not. We went north in search of the truth.

Like most teenagers, the driver – Ricky – drove to impress. Cackling, hair wild, country lanes, tight and bending, taken with bravado, hedges, colourless, black and white, speeding by in our droogish headlights.

I sat in the back, packed tight with boys and girls: rocking, laughing, smoking, chattering, feeling the buzz, the thrill, the 'gid'. If some adult voice had chimed in to tell us to slow down, that we were in peril, that head-on death lay around every corner, we'd have laughed it away. We were at the age of invincibility. Pumped up by the press of each other, we flirted by speaking loudly, laughed in the face of concern at the speed, while arms snaked and slipped through seat belts that would be 'gay' to fasten. We were dizzy with what the night might bring, sights and dangers, that youthful hunt for possibility, a rare thing in 1980s Britain, only coming to those who fought hard to find it.

The car stopped with the handbrake on, a show-off skid sending us to a halt in a small, isolated car park, lights and engine off before we'd got our breath back, all stealth to rare passing traffic. The night and the quiet came as a shock, the only sounds our breathing and the roar of the sea.

It was proper dark, boundless, countryside black, with only the faintest glow of a nearby seaside town to spoil its totality. We stayed silent – for longer than a moment – then, before we could become too moved, someone broke the spell with a faked scream and we fell laughing into the night.

I walked to the edge of the gravel and had a piss to show I wasn't intimidated by the darkness. The wind was blowing in from the sea and you could hear it bumping hard against the chalk cliffs I knew were not far away.

3

I'd grown up visiting the local beaches, their lighthouses and steep lifeboat ramps, the cliffs the highest in the north they said. The coastline here is battered and bloodied by history, both real and fictional. Beneath my feet there had been smugglers with their secret caves and passages; Robinson Crusoe had passed this way, over depths that would one day hold the graves of sunken German U-boat crews; and out there, in the darkness, there had once drifted Count Dracula's ghost ship. 'The sea always wins.' It swallows things up: people, boats, around here even whole villages, nibbling away at the soft cliffs, taking bigger bites on stormy days, digesting walls, houses, graveyards. The ocean scared me, had done since age five, after it dragged me off like an animal in a winter storm. Later in my life I'd meet people who had been attacked by wild animals – bears and dogs – and they'd tell me how the experience of being held in the jaws of something changes your relationship with everything else you fear could do the same. Perhaps this fear of the sea was just like that – to have felt its power, its force, sand pressed into my eyes and nose and ears, spun around and around, until my dad dragged me to the shore.

I went back to the others, who were standing around talking, arms stiff and pushed into pockets against the cold, shivering a little with excitement as candles were doled out, to be lit later. Ricky, who knew the way to the secret place, set off first across a ploughed field. We followed, slipping and cursing at the countryside as only city kids can, until we joined a path along the edge of the cliffs, its boundary marked by an old fence. A lone sign told tourists the names of the birds that lived on the tufty ledges below – white ones and black ones, large colonies you could imagine squawking and shrieking on stormy days, every shelf covered in decades of stinky, fishy seabird crap. Someone kicked the sign down, picked it up, threw it with a spin into the night beyond the fence, an act of petty vandalism so common in those keen to show they're not intimidated by righteousness.

Leaving the path, we moved up a hill, the blacker black of a large castle, substation, farmhouse or just some random squat oblong standing out against the darkness. You could make out other smaller structures around us, a henge of brick buildings. As we got closer to the main building you could sense the dereliction, even in the dark, tell the wind blew through an empty tileless roof and in and out of glassless windows, and that there would be a door, rusting and buckled. And there was. We squeezed inside, smashed tiles and brick grinding as we all slipped in. It smelt like damp cardboard and urine, like concrete air raid shelters we played in as kids, places where giant insects grew and waited to spring on children.

Everywhere we went, there were signs of the war. Not far away was a small bunker, another secret place we'd been told about, a tiny door hidden at the edge of a field where men had once been ready to go when the Nazis came: the fifth column. The identity of these men was known only by the local policeman; the first task of this secret army come the invasion was to kill him so as to assure their own survival. Standing in that small brick bunker, I'd wondered what the purpose was of fighting on, apart from exacting some tiny measure of revenge so as not to feel so defeated.

All inside the building, Ricky told us to be quiet as a farmer lived close by. We followed Ricky as he shuffled towards a space on the floor that was blacker than the rest – a hole, into which he started to descend. We followed, tapping out the way on rubble-strewn steps that spiralled downwards.

We stood at the bottom of the stairs and lit our candles one by one and found we were in a wide tunnel that sloped away from us at a shallow angle, its walls covered in soot and graffiti. With the light came the questions: 'How far does it go?' 'Where does it lead?' 'Is it safe?' Ricky kept quiet and instead smiled and set off down the tunnel, holding his candle like a butler leading his guests into a haunted house.

We followed as fast as our flickering candles would let us, the sound of our footsteps magnified, reflected, echoing down the tunnel and back again. Without warning, Ricky let out a roar to scare us. So we screamed to show we weren't terrified, when in fact we were.

After a hundred metres, the tunnel turned to the left and ended with a set of thick blast doors, the entrance to a bunker. Rooms appeared to the left and right, littered with rusty furniture, bunk beds, a desk, a chair, the false ceilings tumbling in on the rooms like old skin. We shuffled around, peering in but sticking together like cowards; excited to be there, in this secret place.

Taking my penknife out, I did what humans have done ever since we could make our mark, and scraped my name into the concrete near the door, leaving behind a trace of myself, a little piece of immortality.

Laughing and pushing, we made our way to the final room, a giant concrete void, the drop below the doorway of uncertain depth, the light of our candles unable to penetrate far. It smelled of damp black rot. People had once sat in this room and watched for an attack from Germany – Battle of Britain stuff, wooden models of planes being pushed backwards and forwards by our grandmas, hair tied in buns, glamorous in their blue uniforms, while Spitfires and Messerschmitts fought overhead. Someone suggested we blow out the candles and see how dark it was, and so, blow by blow, the darkness came back, blacker than any other I had ever experienced.

Black.

We were city kids, used to street lights; the darkest places we knew were where the street lights were broken or vandalised – easily done by shimmying up the pole and unscrewing the fuse on top. Darkness brought a little wild space in the tower blocks and council estates, a little fear – the biggest kick there is – and perhaps even the vague sense of possibility. We lived at night, in clubs and pubs and living rooms, but the sheer nothingness of that darkness, in that moment, overcame us. We were silent. This time no one wanted to be the first to break the spell, no one wanted to shout or scream, our minds nowhere near our mouths or even our bodies in that moment. Instead they were drifting out on the edge of deep space, spread out micron thin within a black hole, or drifting with the xeno-phyophores in the Mariana Trench.

We lived such closed and confined lives back then, and for most of us the future would be little different, that long hangover from our childhoods – being a grown-up – just about to begin.

But for a moment we stood in awe at the centre of our universe, opening and closing our eyes, seeing no more, no less, as far away from ourselves as we had ever been.

1.2
HIGH MARKS

I sat alone in the small white room, watching the snow build on the windowsill outside, looking down at the two test papers. I fidgeted with my pencil, aware that time was running out, as the wind rattled across the corrugated roof of the building.

Although this was an exam I had sought out, it felt no better than all the others; I felt small, awkward and stupid. The first paper had been easy, but the second had turned my brain into a thick, slow glue, the numbers falling from their places, lost upon the page. Even though the room was cold I felt feverish with a familiar panic, something I thought I'd never feel again. An old self-loathing returned as I pushed my brain to form some answers out of the murk.

None came.

Drifting out of the storm, we trench through deep snow until we come to the edge of the loch, its surface frozen deep beneath a winter blanket. Knowing how useless I am at navigating, Dick takes a bearing and shouts into my ear that it isn't far.

We'd left the car in the dark, woken early by the wind buffeting it on the empty mountain road. Groggy with the long journey north from England, we'd dressed in our seats, wriggling like Houdini to pull on boots and salopettes in our confined quarters – neither of us really wanting to venture outside until the last possible moment. The early start had proved useful in the long approach through the deep drifts. We had stopped for a moment to get our bearings in the first light, gaining a quick glimpse of the wall when the cloud thinned: it looked steep and covered in rime ice, which clung to the rock just like ice clings to the inside of a freezer, offering an equal degree of security.

The conditions are far from perfect, but this is Scotland. Here you just climb routes as you find them, not as you'd like to find them.

Dick stuffs the map away. Pulling on his goggles, he takes the easy option and sets off across the lake.

I turned the paper over and looked up at the snow on the sill, thick as a bed. I had a few minutes left until the examiner was due to return but I knew it would take more than time to get these answers right. It had always been like this.

My mother thought I was just lazy, my teachers said I was a slow learner, then they labelled me as having some kind of 'learning disability'. The schools I went to were filled with 'problem children' and I was just one more problem. I remember learning in biology that the brain has two sides. It came as a bit of a revelation at the time. It seemed to explain why sometimes I felt slow and stupid, one of the school's stigmatised, remedial kids, while at other times I felt bright and intelligent, capable of producing drawings or solving puzzles that were beyond the other kids. Most of the time I kept this dark side in the background, concentrating on what I was good at. But at school that wasn't easy.

The route looks hard. It is a classic summer rock climb, but now it is one of the hardest climbs on the crag, a tenuous mixed line up a steep wall and arête. I visualise the moves, how I'll link up those rounded horizontal cracks and vertical seams, digging through the wall's thick winter coat of rime for secret places in which to torque and hook the picks of my axes.

I have wanted this route for a long time, storing every scrap of information I could find in my head. And although I can't spell the name of the route, or the corrie we are in, I can list everyone who has tried it, what else they've done and why they had failed.

As I step up to the base, I remember the discouraging words of a climber who has failed on this route twice: 'You'll never climb it, there's a really long reachy move on it – you're too short.'

Flicking my picks into the hard, cold turf that sprouts in patches on the climb, I close my eyes and visualise the route as a puzzle, the pieces jumbled in the snow.

I see the first piece and start climbing.

The examiner opened the door and asked me to stop.

Feeling sick and empty I looked out of the window.

At school my worst nightmare was the times table. The teacher would start in one corner of the classroom and go around making each child stand up at their desk and say the next figure. As it snaked nearer, the blood would drain from my face as my heart beat faster and faster. I would feel hollowed out and sick. The dark half would scramble any thought as I struggled to calculate an answer. Finally, on shaky legs, I would stand and speak. I always got it wrong. The other kids would laugh and I would sit back down, thankful the ordeal was over.

Totally immersed in the climbing my brain is powered up and energised, working to its full potential, its limited memory freed up from all those confusing hoops it has to jump through in the real world. Up here everything is real. No numbers. No words. The only calculations are physical, the only questions how to progress and how not to fall off.

Winter climbing is ten per cent physical, ninety per cent mental. If you're good at jigsaws you'll probably be good at mixed climbing. It's simply a frozen puzzle, your tools and crampons torquing and camming the pieces to fit. And, like a jigsaw, the moves are easy. It's just finding them that's hard.

The examiner picked up the sheets and asked me to come to his office while he marked the papers. Seeing I was pensive he chatted about the storm as we walked through the old Victorian building.

It wasn't leaving school with few qualifications that mattered to me or to anyone else, it was leaving with the belief, created by society, that these things really mattered. At sixteen I thought I had been graded for life. The only skill that I knew I possessed was my ability to be creative, initially manifesting itself as skill in painting and drawing. But like anything that comes easy I had no way of knowing that this was any kind of skill at all.

I found it hard to get people to take me seriously when they discovered I couldn't remember my date of birth or the months of the year, always fearful that I would be found out, that people would dismiss me as thick or stupid. Yet slowly, as I grew older, I learnt ways around this, trying to avoid any contact with words or numbers. I left home and moved into a squat near the city's university, and slowly I began to mix with the people that got things right, people I had never met in my remedial world.

Like the experience of meeting people from another culture, I found we weren't that different, and that I had some skills they lacked, or maybe even envied. I slowly learnt that I had to tag abstract words or numbers with images, like a hip bone for a 'hypocrite', and that way bypass the sludgy part of my brain. My party piece back then was trying to remember all twelve months of the year and get them in order, something that for the life of me I just couldn't do. Only at that point could I see that this and all the other things that once did matter, meant nothing at all.

Then one night at a party someone said my linear brain function was perhaps a sign of dyslexia and that I should get tested, just so I could find out what exactly what was wrong with my brain. And that's how I found myself sitting one final test. Wondering if at nineteen it no longer mattered.

I get to the place where the other climbers have failed. Two spaced, flared, horizontal cracks, the gap too wide to span with my axe. I hunker down on my tools and try to solve the problem.

Hammering my axe into the crack at chest level, I mantel up on it, palming down on its head, straightening my arm, one crampon point scratching near its spike, the other crampon latched around a corner. It feels like I'm about to do a handstand as I blindly scrape away the thick stubborn hoar with my other axe, searching for a secure home for its pick. There is nothing.

I think about backing off, about failing, but I'm not sure I can. As I blindly scrape for something to hang, I imagine the good nuts set in poor icy cracks below and feel committed to the move. With my arms cramping, I'm forced to commit to laying away off the rounded arête, the teeth of my pick skittering and skating around until I pull down hard and trust it, wiggling my other axe out as I slowly stand up straight, my body hanging on tenterhooks.

I try not to shake too much.

I take a deep breath and look for the next piece.

The first test paper comprised 100 complicated cubes, with four options for how they would look opened out. The other paper was covered in words and numbers. The boxes were easy and I wondered if I'd been given this by mistake. Then I came to the other sheet and the lights went out. Feeling like an idiot, well aware I hadn't done well on the second sheet, I sat and watched the examiner mark the answers, ticking them off as he went.

Reaching easy ground, easy in comparison to what it took to reach it, I race up a hanging corner sacrificing protection for speed. I pop up on to a narrow foot ledge, a grassy escape route into an easier climb on the left. I hesitate.

The wall above looks compact and steep. It would be so easy to avoid what awaits up there. Plenty of possible excuses. The dark. The storm. I look down at Dick and think of the hollowness of giving up now. I know he doesn't care as long as I get a move on.

With a nut placed at my feet I boulder out the moves above the ledge until I'm committed. I can see where I'm headed: across the wall to a ledge on the arête.

Sweeping away hoar as I go, I try not to think about getting pumped. I scratch until I find one good tool placement on round edges, crampon points poised on slopey holds that look like flattened chicken heads.

Matching tools together I look at Dick far below as he tries to stay balanced in the wind, his flapping red jacket barely visible through the wind-blown snow. The two ropes arch, plucking out questionable protection, but the big one stays put. There should be great fear, there should be great doubt, but all I see is possibility.

The examiner looked up from the sheets and removed his glasses. 'Remarkable. You've scored ninety-nine per cent in the spatial test. I've only ever had one other person score so highly. He was a headmaster. As for the other test … I'm afraid you only scored sixteen per cent.'

The overwhelming joy was quickly crushed by the realisation of how much more important the second test was to real life. Being able to recognise what boxes would look like opened out might get me a job in a cardboard box factory.

'You're a classic dyslexic,' he said. 'One side of your brain doesn't work as it should, so the other half compensates.' He told me the symptoms of dyslexia and the pieces finally fitted together.

Lateral thinking gets me to below a small ledge. Standing on nothing footholds and holding my breath, I tickle at a frozen tuft of grass with my pick. The pick bites with a dull, shallow *thwack*. With time running out, I blindly swap feet, then hang off one tool as I bring the other across to join it. I feel the dice roll. Will the axes rip out when I pull?

My brain does some quick calculations and says no. So I do. They don't. I'm there.

I mantel up on to the arête. I'm so aware of everything around me: the snowflakes blowing across my face, the line of sweat running down between my shoulder blades, a twist of frozen heather emerging from the snow, the wind, the darkness, the cold. My body is hot, my brain burning as I suck in the speeding snow. The next ten metres are unprotected. If I fall I'll die, but there is no time for melodrama: I am where I have always wanted to be. I think how strange it is that brainpower can get me here, but it still fails to do so many other things. Yet I know now that all things are balanced.

On the mountain such details no longer matter. There is no need for words here. With the pieces together I can see the picture. Who needs to know its name?

Hooking both axes on to a flake I pull off the ledge and head into the darkness.

The examiner showed me to the door and handed me a brown envelope containing my results. 'Andrew, with a score of ninety-nine per cent you should find something you enjoy that involves three-dimensional problem solving, something creative, where you can turn these things into an advantage.'

I shook his hand, said thank you, then walked home through the snow, wondering where such a strange gift would lead me.

1.3

BROKEN

With the last of our energy we bashed against the ice-coated door, the entrance to the high-mountain téléphérique station. Snow and ice swirled around us, caught in the eddy where the door appeared out of the mountainside.

We smashed into it again, knowing we wouldn't survive unless we got inside. It remained solidly closed. I dropped to my knees and tried to prise it open with my ice axe, its pick bent and blunt after the kilometre of hard climbing it had taken to get there. I twisted it hard into the metal reinforcing the door. The pick snapped and I fell back defeated. After all we'd been through we were going to die because of a fucking door.

Aaron jumped at the door and disappeared inside with a bang. I crawled in after him.

The door blew shut as we rolled on to our backs, sealing out the storm and putting a loud full stop to the strain of the last three days.

We lay there for a long time, staring at the icy ceiling, neither of us wanting to speak and spoil the overwhelming return of peace and safety.

My hands were frozen and blood covered my face. The rope lay at our feet; new a week ago, it was now a frozen, torn mess. Most of our climbing hardware was gone, left strung along the final section of the 1,200-metre face that dropped away below the door, abandoned without a second thought as we battled to reach the top through a violent winter storm.

Slowly we began to move, knowing we had to find something to eat and something to drink, and to tell people we were still alive.

Standing carefully, creaking like old men, we looked down at the knot that joined us. We began to untie. The rope, which had kept us alive and was now only fit for washing line, fell to the floor.

We lifted our tired heads and took off our helmets.

We smiled at each other.

We would never tie ourselves together again.

Aaron was a great climbing partner. He never complained. In fact he never said anything. I met him at a barbecue; he was doing a PhD in physics and I was working in a climbing shop. No matter how uncomfortable or dangerous the situation, he was always calm under pressure. We'd climbed a fair bit together, shared misfortune and luck, got ourselves in and out of countless epics, yet we'd remained friends. It was Aaron's second winter trip to Chamonix and my third, and as usual I had big plans, which I assumed Aaron would be up for.

Maybe it was because he was coming to the end of his PhD in Sheffield, but he seemed more cautious, laughing off my suggestion of the Carrington-Rouse as a joke, not realising I was serious. We seemed to be pulling in different directions – classic ice versus modern mixed. 'How about the Frendo?' I suggested, knowing that on paper this might look like a suitable compromise to him. He agreed, with the proviso that it wouldn't be all mixed. He didn't mind hard work, but he wasn't into spending days and days suffering on some monstrous epic climb. 'Epics are your bread and butter, Andy, not mine.' So the Frendo it was.

Like many route suggestions, the Frendo was a selfish one. I'd failed on it the year before with Dick Turnbull, mainly because of a British Approach to Winter Alpinism and poor conditions. Although Dick and I should have known better, we got on it expecting an easy winter tick, forgetting that if you came across a 1,200-metre Severe in Scotland in winter you'd approach it with a little more respect. Since then I'd learned that the original and most of the few subsequent winter ascents had avoided the main buttress, the meat of the route, by climbing a snow couloir to the right – which has had the indignity of being skied and surfed the last few years – and been claimed as the Frendo Spur. Poring over photos of the spur, I'd spotted a new line up the left-hand side of the buttress that could provide plenty of 'Scottish action', and I assumed that once on the route Aaron would get into it and enjoy the climbing. If not, I was prepared to push our partnership a little in order to get up it.

Aaron planted his axes and looked up from the bergschrund. 'Mixed climbing, I knew it. The normal route goes up the snow ramps round the corner. There's no direct start in the guide.'

'It looks fun.'

'It's too bloody cold for fun. I'll warn you now, I'm on my holidays; I don't want to suffer, have epics or scratch around on icy rock for two weeks. OK? By the way, why have we only got one rope?'

'So you can't wimp out and abseil off when you're suffering, mixed climbing and having an epic, that's why.'

Several hours later we were back on route after some difficult climbing up icy granite grooves. Aaron arrived at the belay grumbling and looking a bit perturbed. The mixed climbing had so far proved harder and more insecure than expected, we were only on the lower ungraded section of the route, and we were climbing much slower than we'd anticipated. It was Aaron's lead. He eyed the difficulties for longer than was necessary, so I offered to carry on leading before he had the chance to persuade me to retreat before we became too committed. My parting words were designed to cheer him up a bit: 'Ah, don't you just love the smell of sulphur in the morning?'

Looking down the spur, he measured our height by the lengthening shadows as they moved across our tracks. 'Afternoon, actually.'

Hammering a Spectre into a crack, I pretended not to hear.

'Aaron! I'm coming off! Back up the belay, quick! … No, watch me! Try and shine your head torch on my front points. No, stop, you're dazzling me!'

It was late, it was dark, it was incredibly cold, and Aaron was pissed off. So far the climbing could definitely be termed 'mixed'. The afternoon had been squandered wrestling with a fantastic icy offwidth, the evening lost breakdancing around in a mixed couloir, and now, as the real climbing began, the cold Alpine night arrived unannounced without the decency to let me put on my head torch first. Aaron took his front-row seat beside a large spiky flake as I began fighting my way up a three-inch-wide strip of plastic ice running up the back of a steep eighty-five-degree groove. The higher I climbed, feet stacked one above the other, the more noticeable the weight of the rope became. It hung unhindered by protection down to Aaron, who silently shivered as the temperature dropped off the bottom end of our cheap thermometer. Trying hard to keep his frozen hands paying out rope, Aaron did a fine job of tracing my flight path on to his spike belay with his halogen bulb. 'One more metre,' I thought. 'One more metre and I'll find some gear and lower off.' But there was none. Stupidly I tried to gain more purchase in the thin ice by hitting it with my adze, which, to my horror, resulted in the next section of ice falling away in front of me, leaving only a blind groove. Trying to stay calm, focused and in balance, I tried to carefully step back down into my last crampon placement, but as I reweighted it, the ice buckled and fell away, sending my crampon screeching and sparking down the granite until it miraculously caught a stubborn piece lower down. Pressing my head into the groove, my tired, hungry body tried to puke up with fear, only managing a pathetic dry heave.

'Andy, what's going on up there? Hurry up, I'm freezing to death!'

A desperate lasso manoeuvre followed by a Tarzan swing saw me screech and spark into another corner, which thankfully accepted a one-inch Angle up to the hilt.

'Aaron … take! Lower me down, I've had it.'

Back at the belay my whole body collapsed with a debilitating fatigue caused by fourteen hours of leading. Hanging pathetically off the flake, hands frozen and fingers bloody claws, contact lenses deforming with the cold, all I wanted was a drink of water and for Aaron to take charge. Aaron looked at me with disdain. 'I thought we were supposed to be avoiding epics?' Turning, he focused his head torch beam on a steep patch of snow the size of a wheelie bin stuck out in the middle of a hanging slab ten metres below us. 'We'll bivvy there. I'll lower you down and we'll use the peg up there as the main belay, OK?'

I didn't have the energy to answer.

Whenever I bivvy in some godawful spot, I often pass the time reminiscing about some similar horrendous night I've endured. Like freezing at -30 °C on the Jorasses or being buried alive by spindrift below the Dru. I find that this usually puts my present circumstance into perspective. Yet, at that moment, hanging from a Tricam on an out-there, one-bum-cheek bivvy from hell, I found little comfort in those past memories. It was far worse than any bivvy I'd endured before. Those past bivvies now seemed luxurious in comparison.

Squirming, pulling, pushing and grunting, I tried to get my sleeping bag out without dropping anything of importance, or falling off my narrow perch. Aaron was in his bag, boots off and stove on, long before I'd even had time to find my head torch, but not before he notified me that technically I'd lied to him because he was now 'suffering'. Below were the lights of Chamonix. My tired mind imagined the friendly, laughing groups huddled around warm crêperies, and those wandering from bar to bar before returning to beds warmed by blonde Norwegian goddesses. What was I doing up here?

'Andy!' Aaron woke me from my daydream. 'Are you OK? Get in your bag before you freeze.' With great difficulty I removed my right Vega shell. Then, after tying it into the belay, I proceeded to wrestle with the other. For some reason my mind wandered for a brief moment to the implications of dropping a boot so high on a winter route. The next thing I knew, my boot was rocketing off the end of my foot. Grimacing with horror, I watched it sail into the air, then amazingly fall back on to the snow centimetres from my feet. Letting out a nervous laugh, I bent down to pick it up, but Aaron, seeing what was about to happen, gasped as millimetres from my fingertips the boot slowly slid away into the darkness. For a few seconds there was a plasticy echo as it rattled down the face, then silence.

In retrospect it seems almost funny, but in those brief moments my mind came close to snapping. I just couldn't comprehend what had happened. I put my head in my hands and tried to pretend what had taken place was all in my imagination. This couldn't really be happening; it had to be a nightmare. Different emotions shot through me. How was I going to get down with one boot? With only one rope! And, for a second, I was more upset about having to retreat off the route again, losing all that hard-fought-for ground.

Aaron, seeing I was in distress, tried to comfort me. 'Never mind, it could happen to anyone … I suppose we'll be going down tomorrow then?' How was I going to get down without getting frostbite wearing only my inner boot, and how were we going to retreat with only a single fifty-metre rope and a minimal rack? I sat there, shaking my head, vowing that once down I'd give up climbing for good, sell all my gear, maybe even spend the rest of my holiday with my wife, somewhere sunny. Just at that moment a huge spotlight came on, shining up from the Midi-Plan, illuminating the whole of the Midi for the tourists. Aaron shifted in his sleeping bag. 'Bloody great. How am I going to sleep with that shining in my eyes all night!'

'Oh god, what am I going to do?' was my only reply. At least there was no way things could possibly get any worse.

It was then that the sérac fell down.

The sérac, weighing thousands of tons, suddenly chose that precise moment to split from the face, explode into whirring debris and crash down on us. For a second I thought it was my brain exploding, until I noticed everything was moving. Frozen with fear as the deafening rumble grew into a sphincter-tightening thunder, we waited for the impact as house-sized blocks rained down around us. I'd been wrong; things were about to get much worse.

All of a sudden, my lost boot seemed rather unimportant.

Coughing up ice crystals we opened our eyes and found to our surprise we were still alive. Stunned, we sat and watched in amazement as a great cloud of ice particles and debris rolled out across the glacier far below us for hundreds of metres, spectacularly illuminated by the Midi-Plan. Then, rising slowly into the air, it formed multi-coloured halos over the lights of Chamonix. Panting, with heart racing and brain buzzing, I felt humbled and stunned by the spectacle and more alive than at any other time in my life. If we got down in one piece I'd definitely think long and hard about the unjustifiable risks inherent in this kind of climbing. Aaron was right: winter alpinism is madness. Why risk all the good things in life – love, friendship, food, gritstone – in order to suffer for days on end? Kidding yourself you're really in control, sticking your neck out, and for what?

To climb classic summer rock routes that are out of condition?

The rope slithered down from our final abseil and off our final piece of gear sometime the following afternoon. With all my socks on my bootless foot, plus a mountain mitt and a strapped-on Rambo, I tried to run for my life across the glacier, praying we'd be spared any more trundling séracs. Three hundred metres from the face I stopped dead and rubbed my eyes.

There before me, standing upright on a pile of ice debris, was my boot.

As I picked it up I instantly forgot last night's vows of selling gear, sunny holidays in Spain and the stupidity of winter climbing. I was down alive and in one piece. I felt stronger, mentally more able to cope with the stresses of winter, plus, now I had two boots again, I was back in business. Turning to face the spur I lifted up the boot and vowed I'd be back. 'You'll not beat me, you stinking piece of rock.' Aaron looked on as he coiled the rope, no doubt thinking, 'It'll go … but I won't'. Once at the Midi-Plan, we collapsed in front of assorted bemused Japanese and Italian tourists. 'Alpinists!' they cooed, and snapped away. I was already making new plans.

'Aaron, get two returns, we'll come up tomorrow and finish the route.'

Shaking his head, Aaron pushed his credit card under the glass. 'One return and one single *s'il vous plait*.'

'My arse will never be the same. I just hope you can get up this pitch today or we're really fucked. I don't think I can last another bivvy like that.' A few days and another bivvy later, we had woken early, 700 metres up the spur below the final crux. Without saying anything, I knew Aaron was wondering how on earth I had persuaded him to come back on this bloody route. Looking down at me with his face cut, bruised and frostnipped, he wasn't happy. Pulling on my plastics – now complete with tie-in loops – I tried to convince both Aaron and myself that everything was OK. 'We'll be in Chamonix by tonight, don't worry.'

Promising not to be long, I set off up the crux pitch. Two long, scary hours later I was still climbing. The crux section was the hardest bit of climbing I'd ever done, have done since and hopefully will ever do. Sky-hooking, pegging and dry-tooling I found myself committed, unable to back off, to a desperate sequence of footless torques protected by a stacked Hex 7 and Rock 10. If I fell, and they pulled, I had no illusions as to the finality of the landing. The mountain gave me a break and let me live through the pitch, although not without injury. Just below a 'thank-god' ledge my Predator popped and smashed me in the face, breaking my glasses and narrowly missing my eye. A deep scar would remind me for a long time never to underestimate a Severe again. Aaron jumared the pitch, swearing at the stupidity of mixed climbing, until he saw the stacked gear and the blood. He was silent after that. Pulling on to the belay, he looked tired and strung out. I was lucky; I'd led most of the route and had little downtime to think about the seriousness of our position, and what's more I actually wanted to be here.

'Sorry, Aaron, I shouldn't have persuaded you to come back.'

Looking up the next chimney pitch, Aaron slowly removed the gear from his harness. 'It doesn't matter, we're nearly there now. Here, take the gear, let's just keep going.'

I realised that this route was changing us both the higher we climbed. After every pitch I felt stronger and more confident, more and more in my element, whereas Aaron seemed increasingly unsure about this crazy climb. After each pitch he became steadily more convinced that this wasn't for him. It struck me that this was going to be the last route we'd do together.

An hour later, I manteled on to the summit of the last tower. The oppressive blackness and complexity of the lower rock spur finally gave way to the simple white landscape of the upper ice field. The relief at arriving at the ice arête was indescribable; we stood together, and for the first time in two days, relaxed a little. I smiled, not because I knew we'd make it, but just because I was happy. I wondered for a moment whether I'd shake Aaron's hand or hug him when we reached the Midi, imagining this would make everything all right. All the pushing, anxiety and resentment of being dragged on to such a route would have been worth it, wouldn't it? Anyway, it hadn't been all that bad.

'Your lead, Aaron. A nice bit of ice to see us home.'

'Maybe this isn't such a bad route after all,' he said, giving a laboured smile. Aaron led off up the ice arête as the first flecks of snow from a storm blew in from the east.

I still see Aaron from time to time. He works in London now. I know he doesn't climb any more because I've still got his gear. We try to avoid the subject of the Frendo when we meet, although his girlfriend once told me he'd realised that it wasn't for him. He'd grown up, she said. And me? Sitting on some godawful ledge, hungry, cold and nervous of what is to come, I often think about Aaron. Spending his holidays in Spain, Jordan or the States; happy, healthy, relaxing in the sun and sleeping with the woman he loves, while I cuddle up to some other poor lost soul for comfort.

And I wonder what life would be like for me now, if below the Frendo I hadn't found my boot.

And I'd just walked away from it all.

1.4

BOYS DON'T CRY

Boys don't cry, and neither do I. Since age sixteen I've only cried five times. I'm thirty-eight now. I can remember each time with complete clarity, although I try not to. After all, why dwell? I'm emotionally intelligent – at least that's what people say – but when it comes to my own feelings, I'm stone. I put this trait down to the British stiff upper lip, a stoicism often maligned by the overly sensitive temperaments of our modern age. Tears are a last resort. They are middle class. Emotions must be contained or life will fall apart. You are the captain. I learned those lessons from my mother, who, even at the bottom of despair, never showed anything except faith.

A list of those tears:

I cried at the birth of my first child, when the umbilical cord wrapped around her neck and I thought she was going to die.

I cried on the summit of El Cap, after my solo of *Aurora*, when I thought it would make a fine spot for my ashes and I pictured my young children scattering them. I guess I hoped my imagination would have let me live a little longer.

I cried twice – but not for myself – when my marriage broke apart, not much when you consider the trauma for all, and an experience made worse because those tears were six years apart.

As for the fifth time, I'm still unsure why I cried.

I was standing in the middle of the high street of Les Praz, France, in the early morning. The doors of the pale shops were still closed, and my feet were cold. A winter dawn crept over mountains so high I'd imagined them as clouds the day before. The Dru caught me mid stride and held me there. I knew I had to climb it, but I was twenty-one, still a proto-alpinist. I couldn't grasp how, especially in the fearsome cold of the Alpine winter. What would it take? I wondered. What climber could steal this height?

Three seasons passed. Each time I rode the téléphérique and dropped into the Argentière Basin, I stared at the top pitches of the Dru Couloir: Deep, Mysterious, Hidden. Looking over the hanging scream of grey steel, I'd imagine – by pick and point – inching up a twisted chute of ice and rock spikes to the brèche between the Petit and Grand Drus. Youth told me it couldn't be that steep or that hard, but my experience held no reference.

The couloir was first climbed by Walter Cecchinel and Claude Jager in 1973. Complete with hanging bivvies and a haulbag, it was tagged as the hardest route in the Alps; the state of the art at the time. It was now the 1990s, however, and to my mind – full of ignorant bravado – these men were dinosaurs, their gear prehistoric. How difficult could it be for a modern climber? The couloir dropped into space, over vertical walls of compact granite and down behind the protruding bulk of the Sans Nom, leaving me only to guess what lay below and how hard it could be. In the best horror films it is what is unseen that is always most frightening.

Then a winter ascent of the North-East Spur of the Droites made me imagine I was ready. It would be my third Alpine route.

It was never too steep, never too hard, always well protected. But Rich Cross, Steve Mayers and I only knew those realities once we'd reached the top. Until that point, it seemed to verge on impossible: we fought for every inch; it was the limit, the living end. To our ignominy, two parties and a solo-ist overtook us. We bivvied once and had the prerequisite epic descent, but we were Brits and how could we complain? We'd climbed the Dru in winter.

When I awoke the following morning, somewhere safe on the descent slopes, I was free of the fear. I felt that I was no longer a climber who came to the Alps to climb, but an alpinist, and I wondered, as all alpinists do: what next?

My apprenticeship continued, and after a few years I returned to the Dru. By now I'd learned to aid, so Ian Parnell and I decided to try a repeat of the Lafaille Route on the west face, in winter. This route had been big news in 2001, only a year before; it was still the 'state of the art'.

We were out of our depth and nothing went right. The weather was crap, and our portaledge was as stormproof as an umbrella. We'd printed our topo off the internet. The line was drawn too simply to be of much use, and the paper disintegrated slowly in our pockets. We could only follow our instincts, missing some hard pitches for what seemed like more logical lines, and climbing others that Lafaille had backed off. Our second ascent became a first to us.

Near the start, the strap of our haulbag broke and dropped its contents 300 metres down the wall – past a vertigo of seams, expanding flakes and loose features – until it reached the ground. Ian started to cry. He'd already given his all.

I told him, 'It's not as bad as it looks'. I was lying. Darkness was falling and all our bivvy gear was now at the bottom of the route. We had to descend the north face to get it. We screwed ourselves by leaving our rack at our high point. It was the only thing of value we owned, so we were forced to go right back up the wall. Otherwise we could have gone home.

The climb stretched on for fifteen days until the stone, the cold and the hunger wrung us dry. They were some of the happiest days of my life. Afterwards, I felt that I had climbed my Everest and become the alpinist I wanted to be, able to live on the hardest winter walls. The dream of that proto-alpinist standing in a village street was now fully realised.

It was many years before I could return to the Dru. I guess I never lived up to my early potential. I climbed some hard routes, but without them I was crap. I met enough old climbers to know that the lust for peaks can fade, and when it does, you need those other things you'd sacrificed so easily for climbing. I became a father and a husband, semi-retired, weighed down. In many ways I'd written myself off – no longer an alpinist.

And yet, one cold December morning in 2004, I was back beneath the Dru. This time my partner, Mark, was a stranger. It seemed odd that I no longer had any friends left to join me. I'd been told that Mark was a guide. After I watched him struggle, then back off the first pitch, I got worried. Rather than retreat, I took over and switched objectives from the 'very hard' Guides Route to the 'just as hard' Lesueur.

The Lesueur is a spiral stair that wanders up the north face until it crosses the Dru Couloir. It's a cult route for Brits, full of our legends: Al Rouse and Rab Carrington made the second ascent; Andy Parkin the first winter ascent with French alpinist Thierry Renault. I knew the ice-filled chimneys and corners were all steep; some were loose, but always sort of safe. The main drawback was a lack of ledges. Bivvies would be painful.

Halfway up, Mark told me he'd never bivvied before. I discovered he was, in fact, only a walking guide. He told me he'd moved to the Alps to get some climbing experience. And he got it: swinging leads with me up pitch after pitch of dry-tooling and bad ice. The December days were short, and it seemed as if feeling had only just returned to my numb arse before it was time for us to sit out another night.

After four days, the route bisected the top pitches of the Dru Couloir. Since that line was familiar, I chose to take it to the top. I told Mark it was 'piss'. It wasn't. Perhaps it was the lack of ice, or the stone-hard nature of the ice that was there, but those pitches became the most frightening of my life. Armed with one ice screw and worn-out monopoints, I forced myself upward. Beneath my old bravado, this was how I'd really imagined it would be, all those years ago. Mark seemed to climb with ease. I wondered whether I was simply now too old and fat.

Close to the top, I looked up at what appeared to be vertical concrete; I was ready to give anything not to feel the fear. I pointed out to Mark that his axes were still sharp. Mark didn't know enough to offer to swap tools or to slap me and tell me to get a grip. He took the lead and teetered on up. I was saved by a novice.

By the time we reached the final pitch, we were so overdue that a helicopter had moved in; the rescue team thought we were lost. We made the correct signal to be left alone and shouted into the din that we were British – shorthand they would have understood, if they'd heard our words. Much to our relief, we lay down close to the summit that night. The wind whipped up and blew Mark's helmet off the ledge. In the morning, we scrambled up to kiss the tiny summit statue of the Madonna.

I'd given my all to the Dru again, but on the descent, we missed a traverse and lost ourselves in a nightmare of abseils and tottering séracs. I felt as if the Dru wouldn't let me go, until finally we reached the Charpoua Hut and locked the mountain outside.

The next day we walked down, slow and free from epics, through a garden of grass and alpine flowers whose names I didn't know, into a land-scape before winter. This is always the finest moment of a climb: the relief.

Above the Mer de Glace, we paused and took in the mountains. Without the mental din of wanting to climb them, for the first time I could see their beauty.

We sat for a while in silence, resting our backs on our rucksacks. The grass felt dry beneath me. Then Mark told me how his twin brother had died climbing and he felt responsible. He stood up and set off down, leaving me alone, looking up at the Dru.

I started to cry. The tears were still falling as I got to my feet and followed Mark.

There are many routes for me still on the Dru: the Guides Route, the North Face Direttissima, the classic North Face in winter. But the Lesueur already seems like a long time ago, and I thought I was over the hill and too weighed down then. In retrospect, I realise I was in my prime.

Some summits can only be glimpsed as such, once you take stock of yourself and look back to a height that you might never reach again. So now I think that this mountain had measured my rise and fall as an alpinist, and those tears were not for Mark's brother, or my relief at making it down alive, but for the Dru.

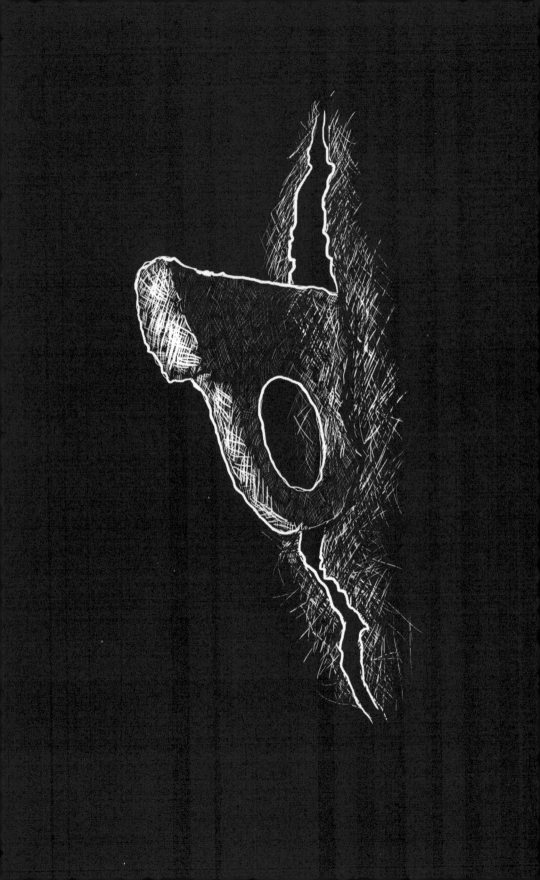

1.5

FORCES

I build a belay for one in the icy mist of the Eiger: a peg, going in with a guilty ring; a brass nut; a pink Tricam; all good for a force both up and down. I check my work, another belay built, and think about that word *force*, a classroom term, a manual word, one that hides the truth. I am that force that must be checked.

Get a grip – you will not fall.

I scan the rock for anything I may have missed, one more anchor before I go. I've taken all it has to give. The limestone scares me; it hasn't the timelessness of granite, nor its security. El Cap loves you, the Dru loves you, but the Eiger? This rock is made from the dead and it shows: sullen, unhelpful, jealous, unforgiving.

The Eiger neither loves nor hates you – now get on with it.

I tie in the rope directly, feeling it already stiffening after two days of winter cold, then feed it into my rope bag, its hundred-metre length my insurance against not finding safe harbour for a solo climber on a face sparse of anchors. I consider what will happen if it freezes, having only climbed 300 metres, 1,200 to go. I've only done the easy climbing so far.

Easy, but under a metre of powder – the real climbing starts now.

I consider that morning's pitches. Steeper than expected and very thin, scrappy, screwless, a seventy-metre fall snapping at my heels. I doubt I'd ever been so gripped: coming round after making it through and realising I had no idea what mountain I was on or even what country I was in,

31

my concentration so complete. That scared me.

It was hard but you did it – and you can do it again.

I think about the patch of faded red nylon I found wedged in the chimney below, wondering for a moment if it had been part of John Harlin's suit, left behind and buried in the ice since his fall down this line almost fifty years before. I'd reached out to take it, only to be revolted at the very idea. Either it was nothing and worthless or it belonged to Harlin, so why would I want it?

It's getting late – stop overthinking everything.

I put on my soloing device and clip it to my chest harness and check my rack; so much gear in order to have the few pieces that might just fit. Then I grab my phone to check the weather. I know I'm stalling. The weather is good and will stay that way. I can't resist a quick scan of my emails – I'm a junkie. One is from my dad, questioning why I would want to try and solo the Harlin, telling me he thought I was past that kind of thing. The other is from my son, asking where I am.

    I'm lost for words.

    I feel tears welling up.

You must finish what you've started.

Then I notice it – I've fed the rope through my belay device the wrong way round. If I fell I wouldn't stop, I'd simply spin off the end of the rope. I stand for a moment and consider it.

Go down.

I do.

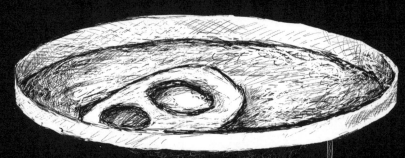

1.6

LESSONS

I wake with a start in a hot motel room in Mariposa. It's 4 a.m.

My first thought is 'She did it!'

My thirteen-year-old daughter is sleeping in the bed next to me like only a teenager can sleep, so deep only an earthquake could wake her, and she deserves it: last night she was sleeping on top of El Cap, having climbed *Tangerine Trip* over four hard days and nights. If there's any teenager on the planet who deserves a lie-in today, it's Ella.

I'm sure for every one who thinks it's amazing that someone so young could find the strength to climb El Cap, there will be someone who is appalled a father would risk his child's life in such a way. To be honest, I see it from both sides, and this adventure has been one of considerable soul searching and stress, as well as laughter and moments that made me want to cry with joy.

I should start at the beginning.

For many years I've brought my kids Ella and Ewen along to my slideshows. They've sat through dozens of talks, sometimes even lying on the stage at my feet, chuckling away. At first I felt a bit uneasy: do I want my kids listening to all these tales of derring-do? But climbing and the risks and rewards of this life make me who I am, and the lessons I have learnt are lessons I've tried to pass on to my kids. Adventure is in my DNA, and so it's in theirs too – they should see what I get up to when I'm away, and understand both the risks and rewards of striving for impossible things.

I've never been a pushy climbing parent and have always wanted to leave it up to them to decide how to explore the boundaries of themselves, exposing them to wilderness and danger the way my dad did, giving them a taste of both while keeping them on a short leash.

One question that would often come up at talks was, 'When are you going to climb El Cap with your kids?', to which I'd reply, 'Oh, not until Ella's thirteen', thinking the youngest girl to climb El Cap was that age (turns out she was fourteen). This always got a laugh, because it was obviously a crazy idea. Then Ella turned thirteen and asked, 'So, Dad, when are we going to climb El Cap?'

My first reaction was 'Why not?' Having soloed it three times, climbed it in eighteen hours, and spent eleven days doing its hardest route and almost two months hanging from it I thought I knew enough to keep her safe. And having climbed it with two people with disabilities – Karen Darke and Phil Packer – I understood what was possible. When you've seen a woman do 4,000 pull-ups, and use only her arms (and nerve) to climb El Cap, you know it will be easier for a thirteen-year-old – well, physically at least.

'Maybe we'll go in the spring holidays next year,' I fibbed, having no real plan to do so.

But Ella is persistent. Now when we went climbing she wanted to learn how to jumar, how to abseil, would ask me how she would go to the toilet '*when* we' – not '*if* we' – climbed El Cap.

Very soon her mum, my long-suffering ex-wife, said, 'What's this about Ella climbing El Cap?', to which I replied, 'Oh, it's just a phase – she'll soon forget about it', assuming that at thirteen she'd soon be thinking more about boys than big walls.

But, like most adults, I underestimated my child.

She had made it her goal to climb El Cap, and I realised that letting her down was something I couldn't do. I had to make it happen, no matter what it took.

The first person who needed convincing was Mandy, Ella's mum. I left this up to Ella to negotiate, knowing full well the persistence of a child is the greatest force in nature when it comes to changing the mind of an adult. The answer was yes, on the conditions she would be safe and that my mate Paul Tattersall would be there – the only climber Mandy trusted. Paul agreed to come if I could cover the cost of the trip, and with much reluctance Mandy gave Ella her blessing.

In life, if you set out with the purpose of doing something amazing you will invariably find that circumstance will lend a hand – I've always lived by the motto 'Act boldly and unseen forces will come to your aid'. So out of the blue a talented filmmaker called Ian Burton got in touch with an idea for a TV programme about climbing El Cap with an ex-Royal Marine sniper by the name of Aldo Kane. Ian wanted to see how someone like that

– a trained killer! – would handle a big wall. 'How about we take Ella along as well?' I suggested, and so the idea was born. Better still, Ian could cover all the costs of the trip – handy as I had yet to work out how to pay for me, Ella and Paul to climb El Cap.

We set a date and started to train with more focus, with Ella learning wall safety, how to aid climb, pass knots and clean pitches, and self-rescue. She would have to miss some school and permission was granted – now that's what I call a progressive school. The months turned to weeks and then days before we were due to go.

And then it all fell apart.

Ian could not get a visa to enter the US. With no money to pay for the trip, it fell through.

Although she put on a brave face, I knew Ella was deeply disappointed.

I guess before then I'd just been going along with the notion of climbing El Cap with her, but now I knew it was more than just a climb, it was stepping up and fighting to make it happen, no matter what.

We'd planned to climb as a five-person team, with Paul leading, Aldo cleaning (who I'd yet to meet, but knew that as a safety rigger – and trained killer! – he would be invaluable on the wall), me hauling, Ella jugging and Ian filming. This technique was similar to a Russian four-person big-wall system – two pushing up the ropes, two hauling kit behind – which while heavy was very safe.

Telling Ella that we wouldn't be going was hard, and harder still when she said that her mum had told her I'd probably not do it anyway. 'Well, Dad, you are a bit unreliable.' That was it; this was no longer about Ella climbing El Cap, it was about a father fulfilling a promise – I only wish it had just been to buy her a bloody horse!

Once again, circumstance came to my aid. Aldo was happy to pay his way there, glad just to be invited to climb a big wall, while my first royalty cheque arrived for *Cold Wars*. The money cashed, I spent the lot on two tickets to San Francisco and showed the confirmation to Ella.

We were going.

And so we finally reached Yosemite, arriving at night, Ella's first impression of El Cap being its bulk blocking out the stars, the border between wall and space blurred by the pinpricks of head torches high on *The Nose*.

We were unable to climb until 5.30 a.m. on the following Monday morning due to our filming permit, so hung around the valley doing very little due to the heat – the coolness of autumn yet to arrive. In fact, I'd never felt such heat in Yosemite, even in June, the temperature being well above 30 °C.

I began to wonder if it would be possible to even climb in such heat, as beyond *The Nose* the wall was almost empty – apart from Brits Vick and Guy climbing *Zodiac*, and another Brit Ollie soloing *Tangerine Trip*, all proving the adage about mad dogs and Englishmen.

Paul, Aldo and I took turns fixing ropes up to pitch five on *Tangerine Trip*, a route I'd climbed in winter conditions with Matt Dickinson many years before and which we'd chosen now due to its steepness – the steepest route on El Cap – which meant it should be safe in a storm and secure to jug. The heat was brutal; just climbing a single pitch left us close to heatstroke.

While I began to have doubts about the feasibility of climbing the wall, Ella was chomping at the bit. She had started to immerse herself in the Valley – its strange collection of people, its names and rules, bus circuits and cafeteria menus. One day I said 'maybe if we finish early we can go to San Francisco and visit Alcatraz', to which she replied, 'Can't we climb Lost Arrow Spire instead?'

Eventually, Sunday came around and I knew we just had to make it work. We carried ninety-nine litres of water up to the base of the wall that evening as we planned on having three hanging bivvies, and we set up in the dark to bivvy at the foot of the wall, dodging two rattlesnakes who were lying on the rocks, soaking up what remained of the day's heat.

How I would wish I was cold-blooded in the days that followed.

As is usual on a big wall with such a big team, day one was a disaster. We all jugged a free-hanging rope for about 100 metres, then I began hauling while Paul and Aldo pushed out the ropes. The weight of the haulbags – ninety-nine litres of water, four days' food for five people, three ledges, plus assorted crap – was insane. Ella and Ben Pritchard were on the belay with me all day as I inched the haulbags up while being roasted by the sun.

I spent most of that first day either hauling or telling Ella to drink, paranoid about her getting heatstroke. The bags finally arrived, but so did the night, meaning we bivvied where we'd been all day, hoping tomorrow would be more successful. The only consolation was that Ella had overcome her second biggest hurdle – weeing on the wall – which although messy for me (she weed on my legs and boots), was quick and efficient.

The following day was better but still slow and marked by more heat and some massive lower-outs for me, Ella and Ben. In the morning Ella had conquered her first biggest fear by having a crap in a wag bag – hanging her bum over the edge with the wag bag clasped around it – so I felt like things were looking up. My biggest worry was the amount of water we were drinking. Again, Aldo and Paul pushed the ropes up and we followed.

On each pitch Ella had to climb a fixed rope, backed up by a shunt on the haul line, inching her way up on her jumars. As the pitches progressed, she got more and more tired – and slower and slower. A few people had asked what I'd do if she couldn't get up the wall; my reply was 'she'll have to!' – I'd never actually considered what I'd do if she couldn't. That night she was so tired I had to take her shoes off and get her in her sleeping bag, seeing in her the heavy fatigue that only a wall can bring.

The following morning it was tough getting her started, but started she had to be, as we had to move as quickly as possible to get to the top before we ran out of water – we were only halfway up the wall. The sun was dreadful, like something out of a science-fiction film, drawing near at dawn and bearing down all day until finally losing its grip just before dark. Worse still, El Cap was devoid of its usual cooling winds. Again and again I kept getting that *Lawrence of Arabia* line in my head: 'There is nothing in the desert, and no man needs nothing.'

On this third day, Ella needed to be cajoled, bullied and distracted up the rope, her fatigue evident. Having done many walks, climbs and paddles with the kids, I had a lot of experience of this, but now it was serious; I found my fatigue hauling the bags too much to deal with. The low point came when I lowered Ella off a belay and she realised she'd dropped her iPod, a gift from her mum and engraved with her name. She started to cry and just hung on the rope at the end of her tether. I shouted up to Ben and Aldo that they should be prepared to haul Ella up the next two pitches as she was too tired to do it. In an instant, she came round and shouted 'No! I want to do it myself. If I don't I'll only be disappointed.' And with that, she slowly made her way up two more rope lengths to the belay. I was stunned by her strength, grit and determination. I knew it was this show of will that I had wanted to mine all along, the inner strength that she had – and we all have – but even so, it took all I had not to cry.

That night Ella fully endorsed the dirtbag life of a wall climber, drinking a can of Pepsi, eating tuna mixed with soft cheese, a tin of pineapple and a tin of cold beans and sausages. I asked her what had stopped her crying and she said, 'I just thought that my iPod would always be in this beautiful place and that was OK ... Plus you said you'd buy me an iPad.'

On the last day the sun finally lost its grip and the wind came, cooling us off as we climbed the last three pitches. A big wall is always like this. It grips you so tight you feel as if it will kill you and you'll never reach the top; then, at the moment you relax, finally understanding the wall's lesson, it releases its grip.

Ella wanted to free climb the last pitch, so I belayed her up, easy climbing in her trainers, but still on the edge of the world.

As is always the case, there was no room for celebrations as haulbags were pulled up and kit sorted. Each team member topped out one by one, and what a great team it was – this band of brothers, and a little sister. As I pulled up the last bag Aldo pointed away from the edge and I saw Ella sitting cross-legged in the dirt, her head bowed and resting on a tin of beans and sausages, fast asleep.

There is much to unpack afterwards with a climb like this – both physically and emotionally, so much it can take a lifetime. To have spent two weeks alone with Ella was fantastic, and also startling, enlightening and surprising. I saw this little girl grow before my eyes into someone amazing. It was also sad as I knew she hadn't become this person on the wall, but in the thirteen years it had taken to get there. Before me was this human being who could get rigged up to jumar herself, carry a big pack and remain upbeat at the lowest moments, someone who thought her own thoughts and could look after herself. She tied on as my baby and untied as an equal to us all.

One thing I was always scared about was that it might all go to her head. But when we boarded the shuttle bus after the climb, the five of us looking so battered, and I said, 'This thirteen-year-old girl just climbed El Cap', the whole bus clapped her, and I could see only an embarrassed pride.

1.7

THE TROLL'S GIFT

My story of the Troll Wall begins sometime in the late 1990s – I forget the year, but I remember the constant rain of Norway's Romsdalen valley, the sweaty hard work, the sound of rocks bouncing down the cliff in the morning mist. Most of all, I remember how it made me feel: the agony of longing and fear, the simple hope that I might finally reach the top and resign it to memory.

I was with the Finn, walking up to *Suser gjennom Harryland*, my back straining under a haulbag, boots slipping on the endless black scree, the route hanging skyscraper tall above us, steeper than any other climb on the Troll, dark and greasy after ten days of rain. I knew little about it – just lines on a scrap of paper cut from a Norwegian magazine – but I could make out a few features that a bold climber might try to reach: hanging corners and overlaps linked by streaked nothings and topped by a wild, slashing roof.

A brutalism set in stone. If a mountain could dream, this would be the nightmare of the Eiger, its north face turned on its head and shaken by the trolls. Over the years, these monsters had taken form in my nightmares: abstract fragments in the clouds, oily manes dripping on to black claws that rasped the jagged wall's rim, casting their spells, always waiting. We were bound together long before this trip. Perhaps their home reminded me of the tower blocks that I grew up in: damp and crumbling and cancerous – punk walls of bastard stone that never leave you. Maybe I just like to hurt myself, but here, and there, where all hope is sucked out, what remains is the challenge to win it back.

The Finn led the way, zigzagging and panting on strong legs, his T-shirt heavy with sweat in the moist air, slight breeze and fog. He'd already fixed one rope. His dream had been to make the first solo of a hard Troll line, but with his nerve lost we now arrived at this route together. I'd also thought

I was ready to solo the Troll. I lacked the experience to know better, having only the ambition, not the muscle, to bully myself up.

If we'd have been friends, I might have chatted while we got ready – as I do when I have nothing to say – and tried to take the edge off the moment, but we were too wrapped up in separate doubts for even fake conversations. The Finn pulled his bright rope taut, clipped on his shiny jumars and attached his daisy chain using only snap gates. I glanced down at my worn-out daisies, a few of their pockets ripped open from falls. The Finn and his gear were far from worn in. I put my paranoia aside. *It would work out.*

The Finn climbed the rope, slowly, his movements wasteful and angry. I joined him at the belay: two rusty pegs from the first ascent and an uncertain flake draped in faded cord. He hadn't backed it up with his shiny gear, nor had he equalised what was there. 'I'll just pop this in here,' I said. I slipped a nut into an oozing, rusty crack and used my end of the rope to equalise it with the two pegs.

The Finn grunted.

Halvor Hagen and Kyrre Østbø had established this line in 1996. It had had no second ascent, yet. Shorter than the other Troll routes, it was said to be more technical, with much hooking, beaking and 'heading' in its 650 metres.

Lead-weighted drips tapped on my helmet. The wall was alive with water, unseen ghostly gurgles and phantom torrents sweating out the storms that seemed intent on washing its stone away. The Finn prepared to aid a bulge of rotten rock. His gear didn't look right: Friends instead of Aliens, clunky fat pitons instead of beaks, quickdraws instead of tie-offs. I could bring my battered gear, I thought. I could lead all the pitches. He could just be the facilitator to my ambition. He pulled out a scratched alloy water bottle and clipped it to the back of his harness. It was like wearing a watch while jamming.

The Finn lit a cigarette.

I sat waiting, wanting him to get on with it, not sure whether my fear of him was greater than my fear of the wall. The smoke hung in the air.

A rock tumbled down the talus a few hundred metres away, echoing backwards and forwards in the drumbeat of the Trolls. The tip of the Finn's cigarette trembled. I began to hum a jolly tune. I hated partners who smoked, not just because I thought they were weak to do so, but because the act of smoking was a manifestation of their weakness I had to endure. 'I go,' the Finn said. He took his cigarette from his mouth, and, without pausing, stuffed it into the crack he was about to climb. I felt as if he'd stubbed it into my eye. I knew the trolls would kill someone with so little respect.

How could I escape from this man? I prayed for rain, or for some rocks to clatter down and scare him away, but in the end it was the Finn who clattered down, ripping out all the gear and landing at my feet. His water bottle squashed flat beneath him, saving his back. He lay there for a long time, just smoking. Then we pulled his new rope and we went back to our homes.

Winter now, and a new century. In 2003 Paul Ramsden and I travelled from Sheffield across a dark North Sea, up an endless spine of frozen roads, and down into the cold crack of Romsdalen – back to the Troll. At midnight, we stared into the black where the stars didn't shine. 'I'm already shitting myself,' muttered Paul, his hands stuffed in his pockets, his shoulders hunched against the cold. We both knew this would be a climb without beauty or poetry.

That summer, Tony Howard had come into the gear shop where I worked. His eyes sparkled like stars, his skin dyed brown by desert sun. He'd been on the British first ascent of the Rimmon Route in 1965, a masterpiece of route finding, traversing blindly around columns of loose rock and up dubious crack lines, shadowed by immense overhangs. He and his partners aimed to make the first ascent of the Troll, but a Norwegian team beat them by a day. I opened Doug Scott's *Himalayan Climber* to a picture of the Troll, and I asked Tony about new route potential. With his finger, he drew a line close to the climb *Death to All*. 'Up there, youth, in those corners – that's where you need to go.'

Paul and I approached the wall in stone-cold silence, over a haunted bridge strung with icicles and through a forest of twisted trees bent by snow and avalanche. The final slopes seemed intent on holding us back from the Troll, their deep drifts sucking at our feet and thighs. If I could keep my nerve, we could do it. Although this would be Paul's first alpine big wall, he was a strong climber, and I thought I had enough experience for both of us; I'd lead it all if need be. We toiled up shifting rock glued in by the cold, hauling enough gear for three weeks. By the end of each day, our hands and faces had turned coal-miner black. I believed that if you had all the time, and the will, the wall would be yours. The climbing was horrid, a dirty job you'd walk away from if it were paid, but my mind never dwelled on the experience, only the summit. This wasn't about climbing. This was about progress.

One evening, after space-hauling our bags, instead of Paul's usual grim determination, I saw only pain.

'My back … it's gone.'

'Gone where?' I replied.

'We have to go down.'

I had a brilliant idea: 'I can haul you up in the portaledge.'

'No, I need to go down.'

Then another idea: 'I can lower you down on all the ropes, and I can carry on.'

'No, we need to go down – I can't drive home like this.'

I felt stung. 'OK. I'll leave all the kit, and I'll come back and solo it.'

'Whatever.'

We tied six ropes end to end and lowered them. Paul threw his haulbag off. As it hit the snow slope, a horrible, hollow impact echoed back and forth, like the sound of a fallen body. Paul looked at me as the noise faded. I lashed the remaining bags to the wall, protecting them from snow, wind and rain. I wondered whether the trolls would climb down and meddle with them. *No, because they want you to come back.*

For months, my gear remained in the possession of the trolls – a bond – until I could unravel myself from the love of my wife and kids and return. Normal life and normal thoughts were impossible. The mist, the cold rock, my bags – and perhaps my soul – were up there, waiting. I flew to Norway. Got the train to Romsdal. A taxi to the wall. Climbed the ropes one by one. Ambition dulled what I felt, and I believed I could carry on alone – no partner to let me down with their weakness. All the while, I thought about Phil Thornhill, who tried to solo the Rimmon Route in winter and ended up falling and breaking his femur near the top. *How hard would it be to rescue me?* I gazed down at bone-snapping ledges – no El Cap nothingness of overhanging rock and empty air to keep me safe. It was spring, and the trolls were moving again, casting down rocks day and night. The sparks illuminated the flysheet of my ledge, keeping me awake.

During a long blank section, I reached for my drill to place a bolt, the first bolt I'd ever placed on a route, but either the drill was a fraction too small or the bolt was a fraction too big, and it bent after barely a finger's width. I hooked, and hooked and hooked, until I reached a tiny shelf which I half manteled, only managing to get into balance on my knees. I prayed for a crack, yet instead I had to make do with another non-bolt – just the 'b' – a tip of steel rod hammered until it warped, tied off with a rivet hanger. This was to be my high point.

The next day, I threw off my frozen haulbags. They shattered when they hit the ground. I followed their tumbling, formless mass to the river. Life came back, inch by inch. The clawing monochrome of wet, heavy snow gave way to green lurching waters, thick curling grass and rough brown sand. A bird called, and a warm wind blew in from the sea. The trees groaned and greeted. If I'd had half the balls it would have taken to climb the wall, or a fraction of the vision, I'd have thrown my gear into the water's foaming depths and the story would have ended, the curse washed away. But as I stood on the banks, I knew that the only way to finish it would be to throw myself in.

A few months later, the line, or where the line would have gone, folded and crumbled in a huge rockfall that shook the valley. If I'd have climbed it, people would no doubt have commented on how the event had wiped out everything I'd risked so much to achieve. Anyone who knew me, however, would have known that it's never about the route – old or new, easy or hard. The idea of owning anything except the experience is hubris.

Five years passed, and I mostly forgot about the Troll. Only words remained, trapped in the pages of my stories, bound by other more positive adventures. Then, after a slideshow, I sat down at a table by a pile of books I had to sign. And I saw him. His electric wheelchair poised, ready to roll towards me once the crowd thinned out. My heart beat fast. One by one, the books and the people went, until there was just Michael, his open hand, unable to grip, pushing on the joystick and moving the chair closer. 'I know who you are,' I said. Michael was another soloist who had tried to climb the Troll. He was the one raked by rocks, the one who fell forty metres, whose body hung smashed and dead to everyone. A brave helicopter crew had plucked him away, almost losing their aircraft as more stones crashed down. I shook his limp hand. *He could be me, and I could be him.*

Three summers and winters came and went. Age dampened the dogma of my obsessions. I tried to find the horrors I needed closer to home. The Troll was just a bunch of slides in a box, a gallery of images online, a troubled dream that haunted my mornings, dark shapes that lurked half-hidden in a conjured mist, an earthy dampness. My children, Ewen and Ella, became aware enough to know what I'd done, and old enough to ask me not to try again. I got divorced and bounced along the bottom of life, where forms of shock therapy tend to kill or cure, and still I didn't return. The Troll was for the reckless. At forty, it was time for fun. But in 2011, as I typed in my card details to book a flight to Yosemite's safe and sunny walls, I thought about the Troll, and I hesitated: *Am I too old?*

'Will you be long?' asked Ewen, now ten years old, as he helped me empty bottles of cheap lemonade in the car park of our apartment building, a converted mental hospital close to Sheffield's gritstone edges. Neighbours looked on confused. We chucked the bottles in my van, ready to be filled by the waters of the Troll.

'Not that long,' I said, watching the liquid foam down the drain. I had no date set for my return; my plan was to drive to Romsdal and not return until I'd done the wall. I called it my 'bastard window' – when I'd stop being a father, a boyfriend, a son. It would be just me and the Troll.

'How long?' he asked. The summer sun shone through his warm brown hair. He pulled another bottle out of the car and began to shake it before unscrewing the lid.

'Not long,' I turned on my new camera and prepared to film him. 'Anyway, you won't miss me.'

'Won't you miss me?' he said, his fingers straining against the bottle top.

Before I could answer, he shouted, 'Dad, get away!' A spout of bubbles burst out across the car park, soaking me. His question was forgotten.

'At night, we hear the wall,' the farmer said, a week later. Rain flattened his grey hair, and the thin Norwegian drizzle formed beads on his red woolly jumper. We stood in the mud beside his large barn. 'It is not safe. You should not go up on the Trollveggen alone.'

His hands were wrapped around a tall walking stick, his fingers thick from a lifetime of labour in this small, lush band of earth between the river and the black talus of the Troll.

One finger was missing.

'I'll be careful.'

He turned and looked at my van, and then he gazed back at me with sad green eyes, sad sane eyes that knew I'd come all the way from Britain for this.

'Do you know of the accidents?'

'Yes.'

'I was here when the English came in 1965. They camped over there,' the farmer said. He smiled. 'There were many climbers back then, but not any more.'

I ferried loads up to *Suser gjennom Harryland*, retracing all those steps, and once more I climbed to the belay where the Finn had fallen at my feet. I slipped my fingers into the rusty crack and felt for his cigarette butt. It wasn't there. I shivered at all the time that had gone by, the sense of loneliness and waste that comes at the beginning of every solo climb. I knew the feeling well, and I waited for it to pass. Emotion had no place on the Troll.

I was planning to climb capsule style, and I still had ten days worth of food and water to shuttle before I could begin. One thing that worried me was that the line finished at the intersection with the East Pillar of Trollryggen. How would I rappel the overhanging wall alone? Would a climb that does not reach the summit satisfy me? I touched the black, slimy rock. I'd missed the Troll.

Of the route, there's not a lot to say. Seventeen rope lengths of horrible, steep and crumbly stone. I quickly understood that the word *løst* on the topo means 'loose' and was saved for the worst pitches, when I felt as though I was crawling through a haunted house of balanced objects that might cut my rope if I put a foot or a hand or any part of me in the wrong place. I fell once, when the rusty cable on a fixed head snapped, but by then I was too high to run away easily, so I worked it out. Near the top, I crept on to a tipped-out cam, the biggest one I had, wondering why the topo hadn't mentioned such a wide crack. To my horror, the rock groaned. I retreated on to a hook, my hands trembling, and then down all my tied-together ropes, my whole body shaken. And yet I returned. It was all I could do.

I reached the crux on the eighth day, I think: a corroded roof of loose plates and overlapping shields. I tapped the rock with my hammer to find what was solid and what was not, playing a tune for the trolls. Kicking and breaking away rock to make myself safe, I had that out-of-body feeling one gets in the most dangerous situations, as if almost every cell in my body was telling me to back down, but some dominant side kept pushing on. Sometimes it's your history together that keeps you going: you and the climb, you and yourself; the parts that scare you, the weakness that you want to overcome, the will to live that eats away at all you think you could be.

With only two litres of water left, no food and two out of four ropes damaged – their sprouted cores covered by tape, I was three pitches below the end. Winter snows already faded the black stone. I recognised this as the kind of moment when any flaw is exposed, when you tell yourself that you should back down, when you know that others would say that choice was the right one. *But they'd be wrong*, I thought. *Most people are just weak, and your weakness just makes them feel better about theirs.*

I committed everything. I made four moves on beaks before I realised that I'd clipped the wrong end of my lead rope into the gear: a fall would have tossed me sixty metres into space. A little higher and my knee became stuck, leaving me hanging upside down. As I fought to extricate myself, I considered the embarrassment of dying in such a way. I pressed on until I felt as if I was no longer climbing – gaining inches, and only by the momentum of my desire. At last, the top of the wall was just thirty-five metres away. I stood on a tiny plinth, everything around me wobbly and uncertain. I had perhaps an hour of daylight left, and I knew that I was pushing way out there, that I'd have to negotiate the overhanging wall to reach my ledge in the dark. On every pitch so far, there'd been two

8-millimetre bolts. Now I climbed up and down in search of a final belay, gently touching the shifting, grating flakes as if they were fine bone china.

I moved left. Nothing. I moved right. Nothing. I climbed a pillar in my clunky boots. Nothing. I stopped moving. I tried to will myself a path, to link my ambition with reality. Only thirty-five metres. Nothing. If those flakes came away they'd cut my rope. Twilight made it hard to think; the gloom seemed to bully me, crowding in on what little I could see.

And then it happened.

I heard Ewen's voice.

My camera had knocked against the rock, and it began playing the movie I'd taken of him in the car park, with the lemonade.

'Dad, get away!'

I don't believe in signs. It didn't matter what I heard him say. It only mattered that I heard his voice. It was real. It broke the spell. I smashed the debris from a crack, placed a cam and started down.

All the way home, the light shone, and the mountains of Norway were more beautiful than any other landscape I'd seen. Rare northern sunbeams picked up delicate autumnal colours. Candy-green lichen freckled the granite. Martian reds spread over the tundra, down to lakes where the wind and water spun and played. You'd think I'd be angry at getting so close, but I wasn't. Defeat was my choice, and it didn't feel like defeat. It felt like an end on my terms.

A lovely emptiness stayed with me as I crossed back over the sea, back to Sheffield and the school gates where Ewen and Ella appeared, their bodies darting toward me, even before their widening eyes took me in. They jumped into my arms. Weightless.

It took me a while to understand what that emptiness was, a space devoid of bitterness or desire, schemes or excuses. I had no reference for it, so I labelled it peace. And this should have been the end.

And yet, as I told my stories of the Troll, people always asked:

Would you go back?

Will you go back?

When are you going back?

I shrugged.

Far away in the north, the trolls must have felt my heart stir, and they recast their magic.

I was still cursed.

September 2012. The sports car sped along the quiet Norwegian road, winding on to a rock-strewn plateau fringed by glaciers and mountains, its turbo kicking in, then dropping off. Its driver's face, wearing a mask of seriousness, was fully engaged on the turns ahead. Our conversation had been minimal. It probably didn't help that I'd made the childlike comment, 'Oh, you have a fancy car', upon first seeing what was obviously an important possession. Or that when Tormod Granheim had asked me what I drove, I'd replied, 'a car'. Dave Durkan, a Welsh climber who lived in Oslo, had persuaded Tormod to give me a lift to the annual Fjellfestival, where I was supposed to give a talk about attempting the Troll. 'He may be a skier,' Dave said, 'but he's mad like you.'

I was still trying to think about something to say as the car accelerated up a road. My knowledge of skiing was about as extensive as my understanding of sport cars.

'Do you like coffee?' Tormod asked, his gaze fixed on the road.

'No, but I like tea,' I replied. Then I realised this subject could have been a topic for discussion, if only I'd liked coffee.

'Good coffee is very important in life,' Tormod said.

'I don't mind a latte now and then.'

'A latte?' Tormod mumbled, obviously disgusted. 'That is coffee for people who don't know anything.'

Before I could think of some defence, the car darted off the road towards a small, old garage, its wooden walls stained red. 'The coffee is adequate here,' Tormod said. His hands rested on the wheel. The engine purred. He made no sign of wanting to get out.

'Are we going in?' I asked, wondering whether he'd just stopped to show me where I could, one day, buy some 'adequate' coffee.

'We must wait,' Tormod said. His hands gripped the wheel like those of a getaway driver. 'I must first lubricate my turbo.'

'Is that a euphemism?' I asked.

It wasn't.

We stood outside the fancy sports car while Tormod drank coffee and I sipped horrible Lipton tea and ate a hot dog. Tormod told me I couldn't eat in his car. 'The worst thing that ever happened to me,' he said, 'was once I picked up a hitch-hiker. He was sitting beside me, when, without warning, he pulled out an apple from his pocket, and before I could stop him, he bit into it.'

Tormod paused for effect.

I took a drink of horrible tea, imagining that they must have hit a moose or something.

'I felt the spray from the apple hit my face.' Tormod paused again.

I waited for the rest of the story. Then I realised that was it. I tried to change the subject, since Tormod looked upset. 'I've never met anyone with such a fancy car.'

'I was avalanched,' he said, emotionless, as if being avalanched was as common an experience as going shopping. 'In the moment I believed I would die, I realised I had money in my bank, but I did not have a sports car.'

Tormod took another sip of coffee. He dragged one toe through the dirt, making a cross.

'Do you let your girlfriend eat in your car?' I asked.

'No.'

'Do you eat in your car?'

'No.'

'Do you eat your girlfriend in your car?'

For the first time, Tormod laughed.

That evening, a festival organiser told me that in 2006 Tormod had climbed Everest in twenty-four hours from Base Camp to summit and skied the North Face. During the descent a snow anchor failed, and his partner, Tomas Olsson, fell 2,500 metres to his death. Tormod continued down alone. I guessed the apple incident hadn't been his most harrowing experience.

After my talk, Tormod told me I was funny and also crazy. On the drive home, I felt we had more to discuss. I said that it must have been hard for him to pull off the first descent of the North Face of Everest, yet never be able to enjoy the achievement fully, as it was bound up in tragedy. He didn't reply, but I thought we understood each other.

'Maybe we should climb the Troll Wall together this winter?' I said. The idea of snow and ice seemed easier to digest than more Romsdalen rain. I didn't take Tormod's lack of big-wall experience into consideration.

Tormod turned from the steering wheel, fire in his eyes: 'I will bring the coffee.'

A couple of months later, at the Banff Mountain Film Festival, I watched a movie about two Aussies and a Norwegian, Aleks Gamme, who raced to be the first to ski to and from the South Pole without support or kites. The story went beyond the typical heroics and one-upmanship of most modern adventure films, and instead became a contest in humility and respect.

Back in my hotel room, and without thinking it through, I found Aleks's website and sent him this email:

Hi Aleks, you don't know me, but I've just seen 'Crossing the Ice,' and I wondered whether you wanted to come and climb the Troll Wall this winter. Cheers, Andy.

The next morning, I had a reply. Aleks wrote that he'd seen me talk at the Fjellfestival, he knew Tormod, and perhaps the Troll would be a great adventure.

I forgot to ask whether Aleks had ever climbed anything, but I hadn't asked Tormod that question either. Climbing walls is about more than tying knots. I needed partners with enough knowledge to try – and to learn safely whatever skills they required to see the route done – but not enough experience to say no. More important, I needed companions who had something that can't be learned from books, or taught in climbing courses: the nerve to go on when every inch of you wishes to go back.

'Aleks is not a skier,' Tormod announced, while the three of us bivvied at the base of the Troll. 'He is a cross-country skier. He just walks on his skis.' It was January 2013, and the temperature was so low that even Norwegian news stations had warned viewers about the dangers of skiing in such conditions.

Aleks looked hurt. 'Well, I was on the Norwegian telemark team, so you can't say I'm not a skier.'

We'd been fixing ropes up the first part of *Suser gjennom Harryland* for two days and preparing our kit, including an expedition barrel full of ice to melt for water. Frozen cascades sheathed the lower part of the wall, their icicles sprouting like thick branches from the Troll's springs. Above them, the stone quickly turned black with steepness. The place had a Grimm fairy tale feel. We seemed to have brought way too much: three big haulbags weren't enough for all our supplies, so Aleks's huge duffel had been added to the collection of bags. The only major disaster, thus far, was the loss of the top of Tormod's coffee pot, which tumbled down a crack, leaving Tormod as forlorn as if it had been the stove. I'd promised they'd be safe if they stuck to the rules, and I tried to diffuse their anxiety by asking them to visualise one of those pictures in which a small child is snuggled up beside a lion. 'The lion can kill the child at any moment, and the child can do nothing at all to stop it, but the child feels safe nevertheless, and in that moment the lion is not hungry.' I wasn't sure what I was actually saying, beyond, 'The Troll can kill you, but right now it isn't', yet it had helped me in the past, and I suggested they should get into the habit of stroking the rock as you would an animal, as this would calm both them and the Troll.

It felt strange to be back on the wall again, making the moves I had made two years before, remembering most of the traps and feeling the small thrill of retrieving my old leaver biners from the belays. At the eleventh pitch, our second week on the wall, I asked if anyone else wanted to lead.

Aleks volunteered, so I stayed in bed, which sounds better than it was; my synthetic sleeping bag contained lumps of ice the size of potatoes. Aleks placed a cam right off the belay, but to my surprise, instead of pulling back the trigger he just jabbed it into the crack. 'What are you doing?' I shouted. 'Do you know how to place a cam?' Aleks looked sheepish and tried to pull it back out. 'If we get any cams stuck, we're stuffed,' I said, realising that I probably sounded like his father. Aleks replaced the cam, clipped in his aiders, stepped up, and then placed a second cam about six inches above the first. 'You need to space them more than that,' I yelled, 'or you'll get nowhere.' Aleks moved the cam a bit higher. 'You'll need to back-clean your gear, otherwise you'll run out higher up,' I continued. 'Just see it as a three-piece belay, and keep adding a piece and taking the bottom piece out.'

Aleks looked at me with doubt. 'OK.'

I tried to concentrate on breaking up the ice in my bag instead of micro-managing him. Four hours later, Aleks was fifteen metres higher; he had no gear in, apart from the two pieces he was hanging from.

'Mmmm. Maybe I should finish this pitch tomorrow?' I shouted.

'How do I get down?' asked Aleks. He sounded like a man who'd climbed too far up a wobbly ladder.

'Place three pieces and equalise them, and we'll lower you.'

Aleks returned with a big grin. I asked him why he'd placed the first cam so badly. 'To be honest, Andy,' he said, with a boyish charm that would win over any heart, 'I have never led outside before. Really, I am an indoor climber.'

I wasn't sure which one of us was crazier. The next morning, I jumared to Aleks's belay. There was one cam placed perfectly between two broken plates of rock. A second cam barely touched the stone. The third cam had fallen out in the night. I guessed it was a tie.

I began to notice my partners had brought a few items that should have stayed on the ground: packets of bacon, bottles of gin, cigars, and a solar panel that would be more useful in a cave than on the dark Troll Wall. One day, Aleks complained he had frostbite in his ass. When I asked why, he admitted that he'd been trying to defrost a salmon that he'd brought along. He produced a block of pink fish the size of a baby. The idea that someone had sat all day on the salmon somewhat reduced my desire to eat it, but in the end we forgot about the fish. It refroze and was carried up and down the route, thus becoming, perhaps, the first salmon to climb the Troll.

On the eleventh day, I re-led the scary roof, my thoughts of impending death well battened down by now. I'd made it once. I'd make it again. Short-fixing to keep the waiting to a minimum, I reached the lip before

Aleks had me on belay. I hung and watched him spinning on the rope, grasping, groping, grunting, as he practised the art of cleaning and jumaring. By now, I was in awe of him and Tormod. What they lacked in skills – I'd caught Tormod looking at pictures of knots on his phone – they made up for with confidence and humility. They could live on the wall without ego, knowing that we were guests, not conquerors or heroes.

Aleks saw me smile. 'I cannot imagine being up here all alone,' he shouted. I felt a pang of pride – and a little worry for my past self. How had I ever escaped this place without partners? And what would a future Andy think of me now?

It felt symbolic, a day later, to reach my previous high point, especially since I was now forty-one. As I hooked the old cam with my ice axe, I thought I might keep it as a souvenir of my stubbornness. Instead, it fell into 650 metres of space, its springs in cold rigor mortis.

There was still no belay. This time, I placed a bolt and equalised it with a nut, and continued short-fixing as Aleks and Tormod jugged the ropes, all of us now eager for it to be over.

The final pitch was the hardest. Not because it was technically hard, but because I didn't believe the trolls would let me reach the top. Frost formed quickly on my body as a harsh, moist wind blew in from the coast. Perhaps it would rain. Maybe the cold would return and we'd be trapped in the ice, our ropes too frozen to rappel. We have to get down. *I have a responsibility to Tormod and Aleks, to my Ella and Ewen.* I tried to focus, but instead I felt Ewen grabbing my hand as he had on the day I'd left. Ella held on to the other, and both of them pulled me back. The wind turned the rock to glass. *Only I can defeat myself.*

A chimney full of grubby chockstones barred the way. I hesitated, scared that they might tumble out and squash me. *Dad, get away!* Fuck it. *Only fifteen metres.* Failure was beyond me, even me, and I pushed on. *Ten metres.* Fumbling for something I knew I just had to get over. *Five.* Afraid. The chimney opened up to a corner. *Four.* Ice grew thickly over everything. My boot tips turned to knee-bashing skates as the corner faded to a slab. *Three.* The slab transformed into a bank of snow. Urgent. *Two.* I looked down: Tormod and Aleks shivered at the belay. The wind grew stronger. More ice built up over the rock, each gust polishing away the roughness. Darkness.

One.

The top of the wall.

There were no thunderclaps, no trumpets, no applause, no screams of rage by the trolls, no pot of gold. Just the wind, and, rocking in the gloom, a rusty old wire with a karabiner clipped to it, a decayed peg and a faded sling. *Is this it?*

'I think I'm at the top,' I shouted. 'I think?' I stepped higher on my aider and peered around. I switched on my headlamp and saw nothing new, yet I felt less hurried. I had to make the right choice.

But what choice?

This was it.

It stopped here.

I imagined my tiny spot of light, high in the air, swallowed up by the starless black. I hung there, my heart pounding. Frozen at the end.

I think about the Troll Wall a lot. The idea of its impossibility and possibility never leaves me. People still ask if I might go back. I don't say no. Part of me knows that a winter ascent of *Suser gjennom Harryland* isn't enough. The line didn't climb through the heart of the Troll or go to the summit. Sometimes I wonder whether there's some wisdom to unravel from the pointlessness. Perhaps I wasn't meant to reach the top. Perhaps when I'd first heard Ewen's voice, I should have realised that understanding the nature of things was the prize – not the rusty wire in that non-place, not the arbitrary ending that came later. Had I lacked the humility, the comprehension to know when to stop? For once, when I'd turned around in 2011, I'd felt real peace, as if a curse had been lifted. I'd returned home a free man, and all I really wanted – my children – had jumped into my arms. And yet, when I look at the pictures we took during the last ascent, in the midst of the darkness and ice, there are almost only smiles. For a long time, I thought that failure had been the Troll's gift, but as I wrote this story, I realised that wasn't true. The Troll's gift, the gift of all things almost beyond us, is the gift of hope.

1.8

QUEEN MAUD LAND

My tired copy of *Queen Maud Land Antarctica* by Ivar Erik Tollefsen is tatty, old, and in Norwegian, but that doesn't matter, because it has been treasured since I forked out a good chunk of my shop wages for it in 1995. It has made it through countless house moves, had tea spilt on it, been stuffed under chairs, and dodged piss beside the toilet. The beauty of this book is that the pictures speak for themselves – they tell a tale of a big team, in a remote place, climbing hard and pushing boundaries. This simple book is a book of dreams, a window to the wonderland of ice and rock spires so beautiful, remote and extreme you could be fooled into believing it all a fantasy. But it is not.

Down in the far, far south, there is a place as remote as the moon, its summits as seldom frequented, and equally beyond all but those lucky enough to be deemed astronauts of stone. I love this book, and have revisited it many times, like the snapshot of an unrequited love, always believing its contents to be beyond my touch.

This book was my first insight into the mind of the Norwegians, a race who are bred for the cold – to challenge a Norwegian in the Antarctic is to enter a breath-holding contest with a mermaid. I saw that in order to be successful in cold, high places one should attempt not to think like a Brit, but like a Norwegian.

And so I began my study – climbing with them, hanging out, spending more and more time absorbing just what it was that made them tick. I climbed the Troll Wall in winter with two of their modern greats, skiers and explorers Aleks Gamme and Tormod Granheim. We spent fourteen days on the wall at an average temperature of -20 °C. During the second week, I found out it was the first trad route Aleks had ever done. Coming home I felt a little jaded by the climb and unsure quite why I would spend so long on such a wall just to reach the top; all the pain didn't seem worth it when weighed against the prize. I had somehow forgotten the lesson that no climb is in isolation to those that came before and those that will follow, that all such adventures lead on to the next.

Six months after the Troll, an email popped into my inbox from Aleks, inviting me to join him and a bunch of BASE jumpers and skiers in Queen Maud Land. I blinked as I reread the email, then read it again. Two months away from home. That was a long time. I suddenly doubted I could leave my kids for that long. And so I reached up to my bookshelf and pulled down Tollefsen's book, opened it, and looked once more at the cold heaven. I knew that whether or not to go was not my choice.

After flying from Cape Town to Novo base, the roar of a week of storm hid the silence of Antarctica from us, where we waited in rocking Portakabins for a window in which to make the final jump into space. I got to know Espen, Kjersti, Ingeborg and Jonas – an eclectic mix, with zero or minimal skills for Queen Maud Land. We practised putting up tents, lighting stoves and packing pulks, knowing that Antarctica is no place for a novice. A tent the BASE jumpers put up was ripped to pieces in five hours; a Russian standing over its shreds announced, 'Out there you will die'.

With no chance of rescue from the outside world, I lay in my bunk, feeling the wall bulge, and considered both our chances of success and of me making it out alive. I could already feel tensions in the group, a bunch of highly motivated and seemingly self-focused individuals strung together by opportunity.

The only option was to make it work. On the seventh day the wind died and we flew in, the noisy buzz of the Twin Otter whirring as we spiralled down into an emptiness between sprouting rock spires that would break the heart of any climber. With a skip we landed and spilt out, shouting, laughing and shedding the odd tear. This was followed by the smack of skis thrown down, the thump of bags, until the fuselage doors slammed and the plane skimmed away, lifted and turned to a pixel speck on blue. The drone of engines faded to naught in the frigid air, then in my mind, the lingering memory faded, died and the silence moved in for the kill.

And then, like freezing cold water, there comes the shock of real silence, as ears straining you try to hold on to something, real or imagined, from Earth. But, with a rush, the silence slips through your ears of and wipes away even the memory of old noises held there. That's when you know you are in Antarctica, and you are as alone and isolated as any human on Earth can be.

On the first day we clipped on skis and made our way up to check out Ulvetanna, a fortress of rock that broods on the edge of the cliffs that spill down on the ice cap. I had never seen such a mountain, and doubt nature had made any other like this. We stood and gazed up, mouths open, and marvelled and shuddered at its impenetrability: stark and lofty, it is a fortress against the dreams of foolish men with high ambition. This, though, was what we had come to climb, and then some of the team would make a BASE jump descent.

It was a crazy idea dreamt up in the bars of Oslo, but now plain reckless in the frozen light of Queen Maud Land. No, not reckless, because we would never even get that far. It could only offer abject failure. The idea of climbing Ulvetanna with such a team as this was pure fantasy: four non-climbers, one climber who could crank F8a but didn't like loose rock or do aid, and me. The easiest route was the Huber Route, which at A4 with obligatory hard free climbing was not really easy, just easier. It was like swimming the Atlantic instead of the Pacific because there would be fewer sharks. The idea of climbing such a line seemed impossible, and to get everyone up it harder still, but then to BASE and get down alive, that was fantasy. But I'm a dreamer, and I like impossible.

The trick I find works best when approaching such an impossible objective is to think of something even more difficult. For example, I once had a plan to ski with Karen Darke to the South Pole, which, seeing as it is 1,000 kilometres of flat skiing and she can't walk, would be quite a challenge. It seemed impossible, but then I tried to imagine crossing Antarctica, which would be twice as far and twice as impossible. All of a sudden, just skiing to the Pole seemed reasonable.

And so this was the approach I took on Ulvetanna. I looked up at the mountain, a huge brooding castle of crumbling stone, and let my mind wander up the unclimbed South Ridge – the last great unclimbed line in Antarctica. A huge barrel-shaped wall barred the way to a committing and obviously scary alpine ridge. It appeared to be the ultimate climbing challenge – bold, hard, long and dangerous. I imagined being up there in a storm, how there would be no way down, either from the ridge – which would involve going up and down towers and cols in either direction – or the barrel wall.

The route had been tried three times by strong teams and all had failed due to storms and no doubt a sense that with each metre they were tightening a noose – a feeling I'd had many times in Patagonia. I stood on my skis on the first day and laughed at the idea of this non-climbing team tackling such a route – the sheer thought of it so crazy it almost seemed that we could pull it off. The gods would never suspect such a surprise attack. I allowed myself to imagine such a thing, a trick to make me believe we could climb something else, but bit by bit, day by day, as we made other climbs and ticked off a list of objectives, I allowed myself to look over and begin to believe that in this dreamland there could only be one objective. After all, we'd never be coming back.

Up and up we went. Days, weeks, pitch after pitch, not one easy or safe – but never boring. I led most, but the others led too, each having some time at the sharp end so they would never feel they were tourists or passengers. Kjersti once said she didn't understand why I had to climb things that were hard or tough or gnarly. Why not just go skiing or BASE jumping? What was wrong with having fun? As we sat in the cooking tent I told her that the greatest experiences of our lives are the hardest, but wondered if that was right. Was this beautiful woman so full of life and sunshine because she only sought out happiness and pleasure and thrill? Was I so full of conflict and darkness and turmoil because all I thought I needed was pain?

But on Ulvetanna I think she got it. I trained her up to haul and jumar and belay and clean, and she became my main partner, standing for hours in the inhuman cold willing me on, never complaining. 'In one hour you climbed one metre,' she laughed once, when I rapped down from a chimney that was akin to being slowly wound through a mangle. Her words were full of smiles, not the resentment of standing there all day where even down trousers and jackets are no match for the daggers of the Antarctic night.

We climbed capsule style, first up the 'barrel' wall, then from a rock garden to the top, committed to each section, unable to get down unless we stripped the upper pitches. Each day, by twos or threes, we jugged up the slowly disintegrating ropes and pushed them out, then descended the nerve-jangling ridge. Here and there were places I prayed no one would die; loose sections with hanging blocks and sharp edges that sawed at ten millimetres of nylon no matter how cautiously we weighted the ropes. Each time we reached the tents I felt a deep sense of relief before we'd scurry into sleeping bags and warmth, knowing it was only a matter of time before there was an accident. I slept beside Kjersti in the same tent as Espen and Ingeborg, who I had become as close to as brother and sister – the lives of us all in my hands.

I had only seen my girlfriend back in Sheffield for about five weeks in the last year, both of us tied up in separate lives, separate dreams, a long isolation of loneliness. But now, with this team, I felt the echo of that loneliness reflected in their companionship. One morning I woke with my frozen arm around Kjersti. As I lifted it I heard the lightest of moans, a sound that caused my heart to break. For a moment I thought I had fallen a little in love – only a dreamland love – not a love that would last. Deep down I knew it wasn't that, but the feeling rose that the love I had at home could not withstand the loneliness. It was simply not enough to keep me safe from places such as this.

The pitches rolled on and on, up and up, passing mousetrap walls and gardens of alien stone, until we thought we had reached the top; a horn that blocked the summit, steep and twisted and gearless, overhanging the whole ridge like an index finger raised to all those who had believed they could get this far. We were the first.

It was beyond me how to climb it, but so had been many things on the South Ridge, so I tried, half-aiding until a crack ran into crumbling mortar, leaving heavy boils of stone to bridge and lightly pull. And then I saw it. Hidden from below, suddenly appearing: a hole, just big enough for a man who had lost fifteen per cent of his body weight to pass into. But where did it go? To the top or somewhere else? I no longer cared.

It was pothole tight, and I wormed away in tatty shell and ripped trousers. My boots, now full of holes, tapped the stone until with a squeeze I popped out on a vertical face of Patagonian-style snow. Moments later I fell, my fingers just grasping a Camalot 5. I willed myself on, against failure, through the snow. And there was the summit of Ulvetanna, only thirty metres of scrambling away. The Last Great Climb my arse!

We reached the summit together and descended the same day. It was the longest, hardest day I have ever spent in the mountains: thirty-six hours that pushed me so far I went deaf in one ear. It took us several days to recover, but bit by bit, we put ourselves back together and began to pack, the last day spent removing all traces and leaving the wind to do the rest. Our snow walls were now rounded not square, our igloo deflated by the sun; what remained would be dismantled by the winter storms that were already gathering out in the white.

When the plane arrived, we jumped and whooped like Americans, and then nervously packed it so tight we feared we'd never get off the ground. Then, one by one, we climbed in to leave, some clambering up like shipwrecked sailors dropped in a net, others lingering, one foot on the ice, the other on the first rung of reality. I was the last to board, climbing up slowly like a man walking away from his love, his heart broken, not daring to look back.

The co-pilot looked in before he closed the door, smiling. Somehow we had survived perhaps the most radical expedition ever to visit Antarctica. We had done it. We had fulfilled the chance we had been given.

The plane's engines fired up and everyone whooped once more, all eager for food, showers and beds. All but one.

'I don't want to leave,' I said, staring out of the window, knowing that soon I would be back in the real world, where I would no longer be the alpha male, but a human being who knew his life would fall apart after this. I knew Queen Maud Land was not real. What we had done, felt and known with certainty was unreal. These things, these mountains and experiences, a place in our imaginations, even if we never knew or acknowledged that they were there.

'I think you should leave me,' I said, my heart breaking. But my words were lost in the engine noise as the empty silence throttled back, retreated one more time, and with a roar we flew back towards the world.

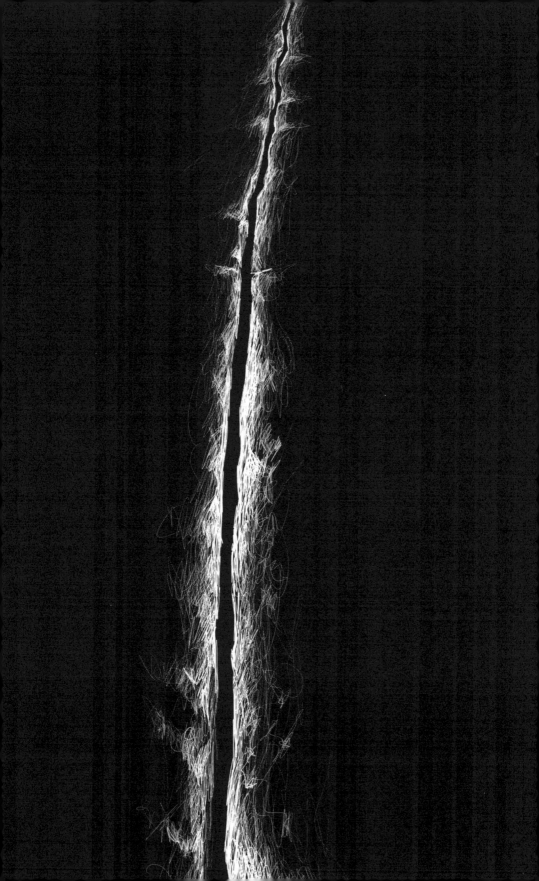

1.9

CELEBRITY ABUSE

Hello Andrew, I work for Sport Relief and wondered if you'd be interested in talking about climbing El Capitan with a celebrity next March on the TV?

I had no idea who Alex Jones was when I found out I'd be climbing Moonlight Buttress in Zion with her, initially mistaking her name on the email for uber-choirboy legend Aled Jones. We only met once before the climb, I found out she presented *The One Show* and had been on *Strictly Come Dancing*. She seemed nice enough, if a little too made-up, when we met for our one training session together, which, due to her schedule, was restricted to a morning at the Castle Climbing Centre in London. When combined with filming, this left about forty minutes for climbing. All we had time to do was jumar up two hanging ropes in the high tower on the side of the wall. I got her harnessed up and clipped in to the rope, and we began to climb as the TV crew filmed us.

Straight away I could see Alex was scared, but she tried to remain professional, stopping to ask questions in her TV voice, such as 'How long have you been climbing?' and 'How strong is this rope?' About twenty metres up I asked her if she felt comfortable and safe and she lied and said that she did.

'How would you feel if it got windy?' I asked, grabbing her harness and swinging her across the wall.

'Fucking get off me!' she screamed. 'You're too heavy, you'll pull me off!'

It was the first time I heard real Alex, not TV Alex. It wouldn't be the last.

There was much to do and sort, but knowing it was TV I just buggered off to Queen Maud Land in Antarctica for two months and left it all to someone else, trying to see myself as 'the talent'. Arriving home, I half expected to read that the programme had been cancelled. Instead, I found several hundred emails I'd been cc'ed into. It was still on.

We arrived in Las Vegas a few days before Alex – me, great cameramen, editors from Belfast and the safety team. I'd worked with or knew most of the people, but as with most projects like this, time and budgets were tight. To pull off the climb was one thing; to pull it off for live TV every night, as well as producing a thirty-minute documentary for the Sunday after the climb, was something else. Many times over those ten days I was glad I just had to climb; the technical guys ran themselves ragged, often sleeping an hour or two between filming and editing. On my side, I was lucky to be working with cameraman Ben Pritchard, and the safety team of Paul Tattersall, Brian Hall and Rory Gregory. I'd been on several crazy filming projects with Ben and Paul, and it was great to be working with Brian and Rory – both legends.

I picked up Alex and Sandy the producer from the airport and drove them back to Zion, getting some footage of Alex seeing Moonlight Buttress for the first time on the way. If you've never been to Zion, then you have to go; it is one of the more special climbing destinations I've visited, and feels much wilder and more adventurous than Yosemite. The walls themselves are much shorter, a third of the height of El Cap, but their beauty and mood make up for this, with the many bands of colour and the closeness of the walls creating a very intense space.

Moonlight Buttress is only about HVS and A1, so the climbing seemed to me like a jolly. The only thing I was worried about was rain, as I'd been told the rock dissolves when wet, something you could test by throwing a rock into a river and watching it melt away. There was a great deal of stress about something going wrong with gear or the weather. But the forecast was good, and the pressure was so on, the money so spent, that failure was impossible.

As with all TV, the actual business of climbing the bloody thing was ignored. Alex carried out a series of live interviews near the base, before a huge caravan of fixers, safety people, rangers and groupies walked in with us. It was Alex's birthday, so they'd had a cake made as a surprise. It had gone into my haulbag and seemed to weigh more than my rack.

We got to the first scramble up to the start of the route, and for the first time in a week we finally left the circus behind: just me, Alex, Paul and Ben. Alex got her kit on, purple helmet and harness, and looked up at the first pitch as Ben jumared a fixed line and prepared to film. This would be Alex's second ever outdoor pitch, almost all her climbing so far done on artificial walls.

The first pitch of Moonlight Buttress is an awkward groove with smears for feet, leading up to a friction traverse right to a ledge. It looked tricky, like a classic gritstone HVS, only on rock that was more like southern sandstone. I tied in and started up while Alex belayed. After a few metres I stopped to ask if she'd ever belayed before. 'No.'

I arrived at the belay and took the rope in tight, very tight, and shouted for her to start climbing. It took a few minutes for the rope to move, and almost as soon as it did, the sound of terror carried up from the belay: 'I'm totally out of my depth.' Out of sight, there was no mollycoddling; Paul had to talk Alex up the pitch, the sound of her terror at being on this holdless groove echoing around the wall. Like most novice climbers, it was as if she believed that if she fell she would die. Finally, and almost hyperventilating, she got to the traverse. We talked her across and she got stuck at the final crack before the ledge, ending up half belly flopped on it as we told her to calm down, the words 'Oh Andy, oh Annnddddy' repeated again and again. When Sandy saw the footage, rushed down on SD card that night, the blood apparently drained from his face; the extremeness of what Alex was doing and how scared she seemed, was beyond entertainment. The worst of it was cut. Otherwise, the whole project risked being canned as people worried about Alex's safety. When it was broadcast that night, it came with a warning.

Alex hung there panting, looking terrified, beyond caring about TV or charity appeals. 'Remember you said you wanted it to be hard,' I shouted down, her fingers scrabbling for holds. 'This is what hard feels like.'

When you take a newbie up a big wall, the one thing they all worry about is not the drop, but dropping their pants. The whole issue of toileting being the crux of any wall. This seemed to weigh on Alex's mind a great deal in the run up to the climb, and I was a little alarmed when she told me she didn't even like going in hotels. She was even more alarmed when I demonstrated a wag bag one night – a foil bag that contains a small bin liner to crap in, some toilet roll, a wet wipe and some cat litter powder (which invariably ends up all over the squatter the first time you open the bag). My description of pooing in a bag wearing a harness, helpfully noting that 'knowing where your asshole is a good idea', produced a look of abject horror, and by the time I was demonstrating massaging the crap-filled bag in order to remove all the air, she looked positively green. That first night on the wall was our first test, as she'd not even had a wee since the morning. I was busting, so sneaked up on to a higher ledge and had a speedy crap, sticking my wag bag back into the silver foil bag and clipping it into my harness.

'What's that?' asked Alex as I tried to sneak the bag into one of the haulbags, having forgotten to bring a poop tube.

'It's one of your birthday presents,' I lied.

I lit the stove and brewed her a cup of tea as the rest of the team descended to a lower ledge to sleep. Alex sat with her back against the wall, and I made her a wrap with avocado and cheese. She had a few bites, then said she was full, an obvious anti-poo strategy. 'Don't you need a wee?' I asked, marvelling at her bladder control, something I put down to her Welsh DNA, a race at one with water.

'No, I can wait,' she said, sipping her tea. It reminded me of climbing El Cap with Ella, and how I'd just told her nature would take its course, and that a full bladder would trump embarrassment any day, which was true: Ella weed on me as I jumared up below her.

Ben climbed the fixed ropes to the belay and gave me a signal. I said 'I've got a surprise for you, Alex,' and, reaching into my haulbag, I pulled out a big cardboard box.

'What's that?' asked Alex, no doubt sure she was about to be exposed to yet another undignified big wall experience.

'Happy birthday to you … ' I began to sing, pulling out a cake big enough to feed about twenty people.

'Oh my god,' she said, looking surprised. 'What about my present?'

It was dark by the time the birthday cake had been filmed and Ben had rapped back down to his bivvy, leaving us alone again. 'Right, Alex, I think you need to have a wee before you go to bed,' I said, fatherlike, a worried frown showing in the darkness. 'Don't worry, I have a plan.'

A minute later and I was sitting at one end of the portaledge with my sleeping bag on my head, singing as loud as I could to 'Surfing on a Rocket' by Air, which was banging out of a mini speaker plugged into my iPod beside my head. Sitting there – trying not to listen to Alex going for a wee – I took a moment to take it all in. What a strange path life takes; how not long ago I was sitting on my mum's settee looking at a picture of Alex in *Heat* magazine, and now I was sitting beside her while she tried to piss quietly.

'Finished,' shouted Alex, and now it was her turn to stick a sleeping bag over her head – listening to me going to the toilet was also too much of an embarrassment for her.

Like for most people who've never spent a night on a portaledge above a jaw-slackening drop, the reality for Alex was a deep, exhausted sleep, and on waking at dawn she seemed like a new woman. I'd promised her the first day would be the hardest and I had been right. Paul, Brian and Ben arrived at the belay, and the climb began again.

That night we had a full hanging bivvy; Ben and Brian at one end of the belay in a portaledge, Alex and me at the other end. It was a cold night, and Alex wrapped herself in a large duvet jacket, relieved just to be sitting still, as I passed her biscuits and chocolate and cups of tea. Again, Ben climbed over, and at a signal, I said, 'I've got another surprise for you, Alex,' and I pulled out a plastic folder from our haulbag. Alex shuffled over as I opened it and began pulling out hand-drawn pictures from orphaned children Alex had met in Indonesia, each one with a little message. I'd been given them the day before setting off and almost lost them while packing when the wind had nearly blown them away. Ben filmed Alex as she talked about each one, obviously touched, tears rolling down her cheeks. The cynical part of me saw it all as just emotional leverage to get the money in, like someone on *The X Factor* telling the judges a sob story to get more votes. But looking at the tiny handprints and kind words, tears running down Alex's cheeks, I saw it as something true.

'Where did you get these from?' she blubbed, running her fingers over a picture of her with a little girl, *Good luck I love you Alex* written on it in red crayon.

'I drew them all last night.'

We spent the last night on the wall just below the top, all a little nervous about what we'd find when we summitted. The pressure was on. It was the coldest night yet, the high desert in winter as cold as the Alps. Ben made a brew and found the teabags froze within a minute of taking them out, but we'd come prepared for cold weather. After dinner, of which Alex ate only a biscuit, and toilet-music time, we got into our bags. I'd spent fifty days at -30 °C in Antarctica, so was always a little too warm, while Alex always seemed to be cold, even when I gave her a hot-water bottle – which was actually my Nalgene piss bottle with hot water in it, not that she knew that. My respect for Alex had grown over the days on the wall, and I'd started to see her as not just a celeb, but as a human being, full of insecurity and frailty as well as stubbornness and good humour.

'Andy, I'm so cold,' the words waking me up instantly, sad and desperate, like those of a child.

I sat up in the dark. 'Don't worry,' I whispered, and pulled my sleeping bag out of my bivvy bag. Unzipping it, I pulled it over her sleeping bag, then ripped open two heat pads and passed them in through the tiny hole in the hood of her bag. Having done all I could, I stuck my belay jacket over my legs, zipped up my thick fleece, lay back in my bivvy bag and chuckled to myself. I imagined how some might think that giving Alex my sleeping bag was the ultimate in big-wall chivalry, but all I thought about was how I could now say 'I got some TV hottie in my sleeping bag on Moonlight Buttress'.

The morning dawned clear, and by the time the sun found us it was already apparent from the radio traffic that the circus had arrived above.

We would be summitting live on *The One Show* with several million people watching. Paul told me the last moves were up a delicate slab, and I had visions of having to do *Downhill Racer* in my approach shoes with the clock ticking, taking a whipper on prime-time TV and having to be rescued. The whole event, all the money, people and hard work, depended on us pulling off this last piece of the programme.

I led off as Alex put on her make-up – yet again, neither hand on the GriGri, which, by now, didn't bother me; I didn't have time to fall. Up I went on a spider's web of perfect cracks until the final slab appeared, a belay just under the lip. The moves were easy, and as I clipped the belay I popped my head over the rim. Yes, the circus was in town. About forty people stood around looking at the edge: rangers, safety, three cameramen and a gaggle of big-wall groupies. Sitting among them was a huge satellite dish someone had humped up the trail, and there in the middle was Sandy, the ringmaster, directing everything, his trademark black polo-neck jumper on, and a huge comedy set of Alan Partridge headphones with a mic attached.

'OK, everybody,' shouted Sandy. 'We're almost ready for the live rim shot. I want total silence when we see Alex's purple helmet pop up.'

Ben Pritchard sorted himself out beside me, plugging in leads and fiddling with lenses. 'Have you heard how much money you've raised?' he asked, fixing an earpiece in Alex's ear. 'Over a million – well done buddy.'

Alex jumared up until she reached the bottom of the slab, then, as they began counting down from five minutes, I put her on belay so she could free climb while they filmed the opening credits, the timing of everything beyond crazy. She put her jumars away, stuck some chalk on her hands, and pulled out her make-up one more time, obviously bricking it that she'd have to finish on a harder slab than the one she started on.

'10 … 9 … 8 … 7 … 6 … ' shouted a voice from above, Ben in position just to my side, ready to film as Alex climbed to my belay.

'5 … 4 … 3 … 2 … 1 … CLIMB!'

Alex moved up the rock, edging and smearing, her face a mask of both determination and desperation just to get this over with, the whole crag silent apart from her breathing and groaning as she climbed. She got to the hardest move and stopped, but only for a second. Her skills as a climber unable to unlock the moves, she threw in a chin smear – the first I'd ever seen – and grabbed the next holds and moved up to the belay.

'That was great. Sixty seconds until we go live again,' shouted Sandy. 'Are you OK, Alex?' he added, sounding quite emotional.

'Yes, Sandy,' she shouted back, trying to control her breathing while putting on one more dab of make-up.

'You've got one move to make,' I said, giving her a hug. 'You're done, just climb to the tree and clip in.'

'Ten seconds,' shouted Sandy, the whole crag going quiet, just the sound of the show's presenters talking in Alex's earpiece.

'5 ... 4 ... 3 ... 2 ... 1 ... '

Alex pulled over the rim, and, as she did so, everyone forgot about being quiet and cheered. She stumbled over to the tree, and, wrapping both arms around it, hugged it for all she was worth.

'How does it feel to be at the top?' asked Sandy, the camera moving in, Alex almost lost for words.

'I couldn't have done it without Andy,' she said, my cue to follow her up, my big chance to be a star, live on TV. But as I moved I realised I was still attached to the belay, leaving me to madly unclip anything and everything, forgetting whether I was attached to the mountain at all as I scrambled up and gave her a hug. I looked around as the questions continued and saw that everyone, all these cynical TV types, were crying, tears running down their faces as they tried to hold the shot. I looked over at Alex, who seemed to have turned to jelly with relief, her arms still wrapped around the tree – I think her arms may have been our only belay – and thought how well she'd done.

Another victory over stupidity.

1.10

EDGE OF MYSELF

My last day, my first 'easy' day, ended long and hard and painful as I scraped and scrambled, tired and tangled, Silent Partner locking and rope running out, on to the rim of El Cap. I had been alone on the wall for fourteen days, four of them on half water rations and the scraps of my food bags. I staggered, stood, staggered again, pulling hard in the still heat of darting lizards and baking dwarf trees with charcoal bark – away from the edge, away until I was sure I was beyond gravity's high-water mark, safe from the *Sea*. I stood there for several minutes unsure what to do – how to feel, stand or sit, laugh or cry – my legs equally unsure how to address the horizontal world again. But then it's always like that. I know the feeling well. It had been my fourth El Cap solo, my thirty-fourth route up the Captain. I know how it feels at the end: the relief, the sadness, so desperate for it to be over for so long, yet wanting to hang on.

Sea of Dreams is a route that maintains a mystique, a route that retains a grade of A4+ – 'if you fall, you die' – even though it was put up in 1978. Time has no doubt mellowed the climb, with several well-known features such as the 'surfboard' having fallen off it, as well as some bolts and rivets being added. Nevertheless it still deserves a Jim Bridwell grade of PDH – Pretty Damn Hard – in most people's books.

Although a classic, the *Sea* is rarely climbed, maybe one ascent every two years, and there are many stories of teams bailing off it. Tales of loose and dangerous rock, runouts, scary obligatory free climbing and bad belays – it is one of the few routes that still has mostly old bolts. Robert Steiner, the German translator of my books *Psychovertical* and *Cold Wars*, lost a finger on the route when a loose flake broke and chopped it off. No one I've ever met who has climbed the route has anything but respect for the first ascensionists; they had set out to create the longest, hardest and most sustained big-wall climb in the world.

The first part of the trip was spent climbing *Zodiac* – for the seventh time – with my mate Charles, who wanted to lead a big wall, and my eye was drawn over to the North America Wall and the *Sea*. This area of the wall is like looking over at Mousetrap Zawn on Gogarth: tons of black, loose diorite, mega steep and obviously death on a stick. *Tempest* scared me a bit, but it travelled up solid golden granite, but the *Sea* scared me even more; the horror stories of pitches like Hook or Book, Peregrine Pillar and the Blue Room, and the expanding belay – cams placed in an expanding crack! – having hung in my mind for years, dispelling any desire to climb it. The Peregrine Pillar scared me the most – these words by Nate Beckwith have stuck with me since I read them online in the late 1990s:

> *After our third bivy on the wall, I took the Peregrine Pillar pitch that morning. This pitch turned out to be one of the hardest, scariest pitches on the climb for me. Starting out with a long stretch of no pro 5.8, I arrived at the base of two loose pillars which I would have to climb up the middle of. Watching my cams expand and contract in the loose diorite, I half freeclimbed, half aided to the top of the pillar. Next was some tricky nailing, with a bad fall to the pillar if things went wrong. A few moves up I started pounding in an angle. The rock started moaning and would not stop! I tapped on all the rock around me. All loose and hollow. The moaning continued. I thought surely the entire face was about to go. Finally the moaning ceased. I decided not to take any more swings at the pin. I tied it off and continued upward. Finally some better pins, then the belay. And not a moment too soon. This was a long pitch.*

There was probably no other route on El Cap that scared me more than the *Sea*. But then why not do it for that very reason? Why should I let what others say or write about these pitches put me off, about death falls from a puzzle of skyhook moves, of car-sized blocks that rattle and move when you nail them, or pillars that hang like Jenga blocks that have to be free climbed, and from the top of which the hard A4 terrain begins? I had come to 'sort my head out' – to reboot my body and mind, something nothing can do like a hard wall can – why run from such a heady dose?

I had already done Bridwell's other classics on this part of the wall – *Pacific Ocean Wall* and *Zenyatta Mondatta* – and thought the *Sea* would be like these: hardish but OK, the shine gone from what were once state-of-the-art routes, that I'd get the 'tick' but really it would all be in the minds of those who had not climbed them. Sure it would be hard, but I'd nail it and come down a hero – overcoming all the stories and just dealing with the hard facts.

And so up I went, a huge rack, thirty-three litres of water and ten days' food that could be stretched a little, years of experience to guard me against what I might find. I was ready for a battle – but not a war.

It didn't seem to take long to climb all the lower pitches, which although not easy were OK with care and attention, and reach the Continental Shelf and the Hook or Book pitch. This was the first 'if you fall, you die' pitch on El Cap and involves crossing a vertical wall mainly on hooks, with rivets and old pegs at the start for pro. At the halfway point you lower off a rivet – a five-millimetre machine bolt hammered into a shallow hole – and swing around until you can catch an edge with a skyhook. Then the fun starts, as you begin a game of chess with the rock, hooking further and further right, stepping high with hooks on tiny nicks and edges, searching for the next hook. You slowly get to the point that if you fall you will fall into the corner around thirty metres below. Luckily, protection is at hand halfway to the belay in the form of a nest of copperheads.

Unluckily, when I reached them I saw that all but one had fallen out. Getting out my heads I tried to replace them, but the depth of these heads is as shallow and ill-defined as if you pressed a matchstick into some clay. Fortunately there is a solid flake beside them, so I backed up the heads with a 'bomber' sky hook held down by my Fish tag bag (funny but I actually believed this to be true at the time). From there you press on – you never weight the heads; they're only there for 'pro' – hooking further and further, hoping you don't go the wrong way and end up 'in the book'. And there's the belay. It's done.

It's boring to describe every pitch, but I doubt I've climbed a route so sustained and mentally exhausting, an experience probably not helped by being alone. I was out of condition at the start and my hands swelled up so much I couldn't get my gloves on; I just had to hope the speed with which they healed was greater than the pain. Again and again I got to a point where I could not puzzle out how to progress – one time I had to rap off and try again the next day – but each time I solved the puzzle by following my big-wall motto: *If in doubt: get high.* Yet over and over again I found myself top-stepping on some placement that defied reason to hold.

The days were hot and often still and windless deep within the womb of the North America Wall, and three litres a day was pushing it. I found no easy pitches, forcing me to get up at dawn and climb into the dark, the punishment and stress unrelenting, but I could not stop – I had to get to the top before I ran out of water.

And then one morning I woke up to find myself at the foot of the Peregrine Pillar. Again I won't go into blow by blow details, only to say it begins with an unprotected traverse on creaky flakes where if you fell you'd probably break your legs as you swung down on to the North America Wall. Then you reach the pillars, a set of high blocks sitting on top of each other, that look as if they would simply topple off if you laybacked them. Half aiding – with nuts not cams, so as to limit the chances of prising the blocks over – and half free climbing (I call it 'fraid' climbing), I made my way up this tottering nightmare, unsure if it was C1 5.8 or C4 XS. Then with a careful mantel I was standing on top of the pillar, the rest of the pitch before me – A4 climbing with the pillar to hit if I fucked up.

The Blue Room was special; the wall was getting looser and looser, the very skin of it overlaid with cardboard-thin flakes that flexed and grated against my toes, flakes I feared would fracture and sail down and cut my rope. Any pin placed felt as if it could unlock the whole wall and cause it to fall down – the entire feature held on a hair trigger. Up there in the black rock nothing was safe – especially me, my lines getting hung up again and again on downward-pointing teeth of rock. Again and again I asked for a break – but never was one forthcoming, the easy snap of a portaledge corner or my finger finding an edge all I was given. Again and again I would find myself laughing at what I was forced to do: a hook tied to my hammer for a blind hook move out of reach, a cam hook behind a flake as thin as bone china, opposed beaks in a horizontal crack crowded with broken RURP tips.

My food ran out, my water was low. It was my forty-fourth birthday and my birthday tea was a packet of M&M's and the final brew of tea before my gas ran out. It felt like a feast, me of all people, forty-four years old and still alive and out here in the middle of the *Sea*. My body grew thinner and harder, got strong like it does on a wall, then broke down, like it does on a wall. I slept with my arms above my head, as if I was surrendering, the only way to stop my hands feeling as if they were going to burst.

And then I was almost there – three pitches of the North America Wall: the end of the *Sea*. An easy day I thought. But alone nothing is easy.

And so I stood there, fourteen days on, at the end – again. A year older, but not the man who started, with all his doubts and thoughts and old troubles. I was broken down by the wall – skin and bone and fat and brain and thought rendered to junk by the toil of it all. I stood there and looked around, feeling the feeling you get at the end of all such adventures as this, at the rim of the wall, at the edge of myself.

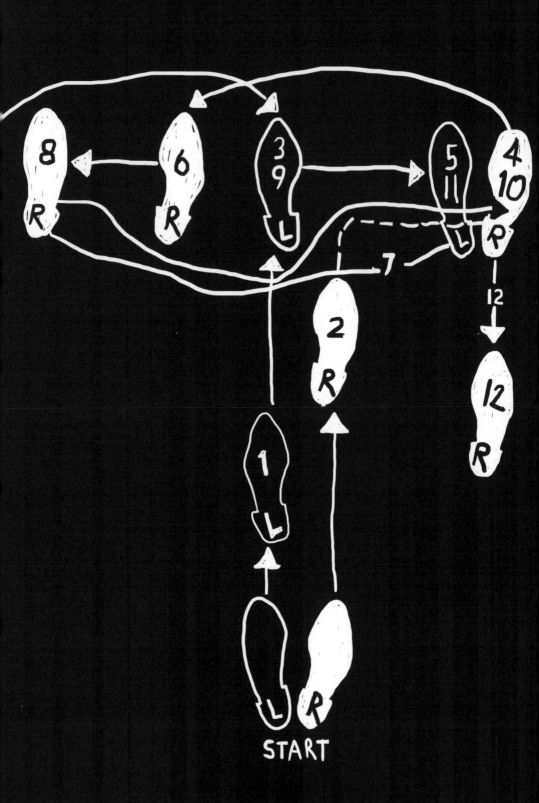

I.II

PIZZA

I'm sitting in a diner in El Portal, California, stuffing my face – my second lunch of the day, trying to load up on carbs for tomorrow. My dream of soloing Yosemite's sixteen-pitch *Zodiac* keeps being derailed, and instead of starting that in the morning I've agreed to climb El Cap in a day with twelve-year-old-looking Calum Muskett, putting aside my solitary and harsh solo dream for something more human, and maybe more fun – well, type-II fun. We're doing *Lurking Fear*, and if we pull it off that will be two grade-V walls in three days, a fair trade for *Zodiac*. Maybe.

Yesterday I woke up at 4 a.m. beside two strangers – Andy and Stefan, the big-wall virgins. Menna had spotted them on the DMM website, two super-keen students training for Yosemite, both with big wall dreams. Watching their videos, I was impressed by their enthusiasm and sense of fun, hauling bags and sleeping in a portaledge in quarries; they reminded me of how I'd done many of the same things.

Acting on impulse, I'd emailed them to wish them luck, and said as a bit of a throwaway that 'maybe we could team up and do something', knowing that as I would only be in Yosemite a week I wouldn't have time.

I kept an eye out for the guys and saw all their training had paid off when they climbed El Cap in the first week via *Triple Direct*. People often talk the talk about just arriving and jumping on the Captain, but few actually do and even fewer stay on to the top. Andy and Stefan did.

Within an hour of arriving in the Valley I'd bumped into them, and as soon as they saw me they said, 'We've been waiting for you!' My plan was to spend three days resting, then go for a one-day solo of *Zodiac*, but now I realised I'd have to put my own project aside and do something with Andy and Stefan, otherwise I'd just look like a jerk.

But what to do? Only the week before I'd had a long email from my friend Paul Tattersall, one of the few people who seems to put up with my Howard Hughes tendency to lock myself away. Like a true friend, Paul never stops knocking:

> *Yosemite sounds good, El Cap in a day, as long as you are being you and not chasing the dream, being you alongside the thousands of other people climbing El Cap … and then getting old and infirm, watching rather than doing. The things we do in life … the shit things we do … drink too much tea and all that. Like you, I have had a lot of intense climbing moments when you have been there frozen in time (so it seemed) unable to move because you imagined that if you did that was it, you would fall to your death, hundreds of feet on to some rocks that had been innocuous enough earlier walking over them but would now smash every bone in my body. No one saw me unable to stop myself crying with self-pity, so scared and angry. Then calmness really comes and you climb, I survived but learnt nothing and can't joyfully share those memories with anyone, not like all the great times Angela and I have had together doing stuff that stressed us but wasn't going to kill us, shared experiences that live on for us. I like sharing, intensity is for losers. What you do works, get hold of some novices and have them along to complicate but share the scene, meanwhile you are soloing??*

I looked at Andy and Stefan – if they had been dogs their tongues would have been out and their tails wagging – and I thought about Paul's words. I'd never climbed with these guys; they had been novices only a few weeks before. What to do?

'Fancy having a go at the west face of Leaning Tower in a day?' I asked.

The west face is a grade-V (5.7, C2F) wall, eleven pitches long and *super steep* – it's said to be the steepest wall in North America and usually takes three days. I'd tried to solo it in a day in June and had bailed from the seventh pitch, so I knew the start, but even so, doing it in a day with two young strangers … ?

'Wow, that would be cool!' they said.

And so at 4 a.m. the alarm sounded and we stepped off, me releading in the dark the seven pitches I'd climbed before, feeling the jet lag and a bit of flu. Doing the route in a day would either kill me or cure me.

'We have to get down in time for a pizza' became our motto, a crazy idea, really, as just staggering back to the car at 4 a.m. should have been good enough for us, but then maybe the magic of Yosemite – the possibility – was inside us. Passing one party – who we had just woken up – we pushed on up the wall. By 10 a.m. I was beginning to feel the strain but didn't want to hand over the lead to Andy and Stefan, after all, they been more used to doing three pitches a day only a week before, but by noon I was done. They jugged up and I handed over the rack to Andy and he was off, shouting 'ropes fixed' only forty-five minutes later. Stefan's lead came next and off he shot up yet another steep crack. Sitting there watching them work so hard, I felt a real sense of pride in both them and myself, that when you believe in people, and commit to them, they can do the most amazing things. They trusted me enough to trust my belief in them.

I recently decided I had to start dealing with certain issues to do with how I view myself and my relationships with the people around me. My demons. I made a list of the things I thought I could deal with, one of which was to give myself as much trust, respect and hope that I give others, something I had become so good at over the last few years. Whenever I'd set the bar impossibly high for others and said, 'Jump, I know you can,' they always did. In fact, most times they never even saw the bar. But I see the bar – it is always there, unjumpable. But I'm changing that.

Like all great speed ascents, the power and the energy of our combined desire and friendship suddenly had us at the top, and not in the dark, either, but within twelve hours of leaving the ground. A huge thunderstorm was rolling in, a difficult and dangerous descent yet to come, but instead of worrying we looked down and Andy said, 'three and a half hours till the pizza deck closes!' – and we set off like friends who'd climbed together not for hours but decades.

As for making it down for the pizza? Of course we did, and afterwards Andy said this had been one of the best days of his life, I thought it fitting to pay for it too, because their belief had made this a day that I'd remember also.

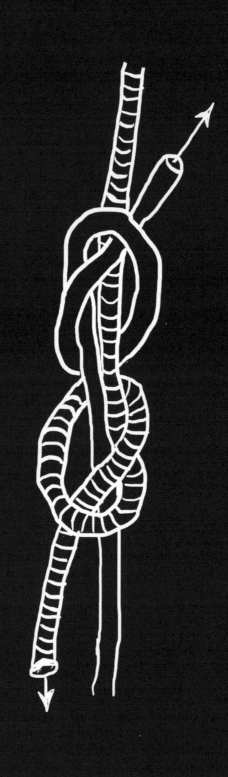

1.12

NO BETTER KNOT

Vanessa woke me early, the predawn summit light creeping in even with my head still tucked inside our home-made two-person sleeping bag, the material damp and reeking after ten days on the wall, the wall which was now below us. 'Let's walk to the summit and see the sun come up,' she whispered in my ear, a soft Irish nag to my leave-me-be groaning, my forty-four-year-old body stiff after a night on the ground.

'Christ, where do you get your energy?' I mumbled into the warm fabric. Most people who'd just climbed El Cap would be wiped out for a week and in no need of a dawn hike through winter snow. But then Vanessa is like a switch, she is either on or off, and after a year together I knew she would not be satiated by a lie-in in a stinky bed. I opened one eye to buy some time as she moved her body over mine, her rock-star hair cast over me, cloud crazy, raining down, touching my face, more animal than human.

'Wake up, Polar Bear,' she nagged on, squeezing my nose, her movements releasing the shared warmth of the bag, the winter trickling in, making this hard man whimper. 'I want to see the sun come up with you,' she persisted, 'but I'll go by myself if you don't want to come.' She knew I wouldn't let her go alone – that I'd let myself down if I did.

I'd been to the top of El Cap too many times to remember, dragged my shit up here feeling both like a victor and a man shipwrecked, shared these bushes and flat spaces with so many people that now it was just camping. Yet I remembered that there had been magic, a magic that I found now only through the prism of another's eyes: the rocks, the trees, the pine cones, the piles of stones, the air, the deep satisfaction of standing atop this crucible of desire and hard work. Then another thought popped into my head, a desire to do something, a commitment to make, an opportunity and an offer that could not be squandered by sleep. This was no ordinary morning, and this woman no ordinary partner.

'OK, I'm coming,' I grunted, carefully forcing my body to move to show it was no bluff; my stiff spine felt like it might snap if I was too keen. 'I need a cup of tea.'

'You can have one when we come back,' she said. I slipped my arm out of the bag and opened my other eye and saw her smiling lips, chapped by the cold, the rest of her face hidden by hair. I reached out and tried to syphon some of her energy, but she jumped out of the bag and began pulling on her shoes. The chill flooded in like a tsunami, and I remembered that I needed to find my knife and a small length of three-mil cord. 'We need to be quick,' she called with a kick to my back, adding, 'you said I'd be knackered this morning, but I feel grand.'

For most men my age, the idea of sharing your life with a woman thirteen years younger seems like a fantasy, but to be honest, it's not. It often makes you feel twice as old, twice as stiff and twice as slow, like all you want is a pipe and slippers, life feeling like you're Frank Sinatra's Von Ryan chasing after that train, only to be gunned down on the tracks.

I first met Vanessa in 2014 at Trinity College in Dublin, where I'd come to speak. That same night I also met Cian O'Leary for the first time, a rough-looking guy who was waiting for us at the entrance. Cian appeared out of place in his trainers and hoodie and baseball cap, among all that middle-class down and fleece and denim. I can't remember what we said to each other that evening, Cian and me, because I was quite distracted – by life crap, and also by this wittering woman Vanessa who'd invited me to speak. She had also asked Bear Grylls to talk that night, but I was £139,000 cheaper, and so now she was leading me to the pub while regaling me with stories about her love for BG. It turned out to be an auspicious night for all of us.

Several months later I met Cian again while climbing at a quarry in Dublin, Vanessa and me at the start of something special. These days, people often ask what would have happened if I'd never met V; I have no reply. All I know is at that time of my life I was slowly succumbing to a poison and I was lucky enough to find the one person in the world who had an antidote. Vanessa reintroduced me to what climbing is all about – what life is all about – the simple act of living, just that and no more. Climbing did not have to be about danger and suffering and going big, but about fun and movement and dreaming small. I climbed more in that year than I had in the previous ten. I loved going to the quarry, and on that day while I was standing there belaying Vanessa, I saw a dodgy character in a tracksuit and baseball cap lurking around the base of the cliffs, looking up to no good. 'Oh, hi, Cian!' Vanessa shouted from halfway up the climb.

It turned out that my first impressions of Cian were not so far off. It's not for me to tell his story, but let's just say he had a very rough passage through his teenage years. His route to rock had been unconventional, a day's climbing after six months of rehab suddenly giving his life new meaning. In the two years since Cian had gone straight, working in an ice-cream shop beside the sea, he'd been pushing his grade and getting good results in indoor competitions. Most climbers you meet these days are either students or professionals – you don't meet too many selling ice cream for minimum wage. I recognised straight away that Cian was someone I'd remember, a guy with charisma and charm and a good heart, even if maybe he didn't know it himself back then.

The next time we met was down at a climbing wall, sitting on a couch drinking tea. Cian said it must be amazing to climb a big wall, that his mind boggled at the very idea of being up on a face for days and days. The longest multi-pitch route he'd ever done was eighty metres.

'Why don't we go and climb El Cap together?' I asked. As usual, not thinking it through.

'Are you fucking joking?' he replied, and I guess I wasn't.

And so there we were: me, Cian, Vanessa and her friend Sinead, below *The Nose* in March, only one of us having any clue what we were doing – they'd done one session at the wall aiding on bolts and jugging and that was it. I guess climbing with inexperienced teams had become my thing over the last few years, something I get a kick out of, but shortly after we started up the wall I began to worry that I'd pushed things too far this time.

Going for the Russian technique of learning by doing, I chucked the three of them at the first four pitches of *The Nose* – usually an afternoon's work, now two days of scary tutorials. It took another full day to fix and get our three haulbags up to Sickle Ledge for their first ever night on portaledges. Our glacial pace became apparent when Erik Sloan and partner shot past us at 7 a.m., having taken thirty minutes to climb what had taken us two days. But we were not after any records. We had a ton of food and five litres of red wine. We were going for a Harding-style ascent, and for every trough of fear or anger or frustration there was a wave of laughter, friendship and love.

The climbing progressed, the winter days short, the three of them learning how to jug, lead, clean and haul on a real wall. *The Nose* is far more complex to clean and haul than much harder routes. It's fair to say that everyone was hard-pressed and I keenly felt under pressure to keep them all safe. I'm embarrassed to say that at times I lost it with people; Vanessa later told me she saw a side of me she'd never seen before, and could understand why I'd chosen not to climb with some people more than once.

There was a big storm coming through midweek and instead of wasting time waiting for it to pass, I wanted to push up to El Cap Tower and sit it out. This added an extra level of stress since most big wallers don't head up with the intention of getting hammered. Our slow pace wasn't helped by the fact I did no leading, leaving it to them to deal with the sharp end so they wouldn't feel like they were being guided up the route. I limited my comments to such things as, 'If you fall now you'll die, Vanessa,' as I watched her place two cams twenty metres apart. Vanessa's lead up to Dolt Tower in the dark was a long one. By the time I cleaned the pitch and reached her, it was 1.30 a.m. When I asked her what time she thought it was, she replied, '10.30?'

We made it to El Cap Tower the day of the storm, but not before I made Vanessa cry and lost it with everyone, telling them they could not just switch off and be passengers or tourists but had to become a team and help each other. Immediately afterwards, of course, I flipped my anger at myself for having too high an ambition for people with zero big-wall experience.

The storm arrived on time and gave us a good pummeling – wind, snow, rain – but we stayed pretty comfortable, having taken enough kit for an ascent of Trango Towers in Pakistan. I teased Vanessa about holding my hand tight as our ledge lurched in the dark, as if we were at sea rather than bolted to granite.

A week in, it seemed best that I start to do a bit of leading, and so I tackled the Texas Flake as ice fell on us from the summit. I asked Vanessa if she wanted to do the thirty-metre King Swing pendulum, quite an offer for someone who'd only been climbing two years and had never been this high before. 'No, you do it,' she replied, but I pressed her, knowing she'd get a lot out of it. I saw an uncharacteristic hesitation – a little fear, a little doubt – as I passed her a Camalot 4, no haul line but just the lead.

'You'll be OK,' I said as I lowered her past the toe of the Boot and on to the wall below. Hesitant at first, she slowly began to swing, walking then running back and forth on one of the greatest and most fun pitches of climbing on the planet. After ten minutes of working it out – I've seen teams take all day to do this pitch – she ran and grabbed some crimps and hung there sideways, trying to squeeze out the inches, heading across a blank wall to a crack around the corner. She looked like Tommy Caldwell on the *Dawn Wall* as she clung on for all she was worth, getting closer and closer … before she slipped and crashed back across the wall, smashing into a corner. She hung silent for a while clutching her side, winded.

'I can't do it,' she shouted back, dejected.

We rapped back down to El Cap Tower, leaving the swing for the next day.

Over tea, I asked, 'Do I push you too hard? Maybe I don't know you as well as I think I do? Maybe you're not as brave as I think you are?' It was a strange conversation that made me question if I really knew her at all. Maybe that boldness I saw in her was simply a reflection of mine. Maybe she was only giving me the woman I wanted. Maybe it was all an act.

The next morning we packed up the camp and hauled all the bags to the top of Boot Flake. Vanessa put on her rock boots and chalk bag and tied on for another go. Down she went, slack given in inches until she found the sweet spot, a hard run to some sidepulls and micro edges, a whizz-bang double dyno to get into position. The three of us looked over the edge as Vanessa hit the right holds and hung on, inching across the wall, closer, closer, until with an outstretched arm she palmed an angle change – only ten or twenty degrees, but like a jug on that sideways wall. With a careful pull, she rounded the wall and reached the crack. When I rapped down to her to do the next pitch, I knew no act could have seen anyone across that wall.

Up we went for days more, arriving late most nights, bags and ledges sorted with tired bodies, the odd night when people appeared ready to snap. One thing the climb taught me is that people do not learn anything until you leave them alone to do so, that being paranoid and micromanaging undermines the whole team. On the final two days I led, short-fixing while the three of them cleaned and hauled and sorted out the mess. Time and again I would look down at mini disasters – stuck ropes, stuck bags, tangled lines – but each time I bit my tongue and shit got sorted. My own harsh shouts – out of fear for them, mainly – is not a sound I want to hear, and day by day they faded away. My heart leapt with pride when I heard a whoop of joy from Sinead and Vanessa as the haulbags reached the belay, or when I saw Cian's smile as he manoeuvred himself through a tricky section of lower-outs. We became a team, the tip of the spear.

We had joked that Cian could try the 5.12 finish to *The Nose* and if he refused he'd have to do it in his underwear, but with storm clouds gathering and our food gone, the flat so close, I pushed on, arriving as the sun set. There I sat, shouting into the night, 'ropes fixed!', shivering and praying with all my heart they'd not fuck up now. And then there they were, Cian and Sinead first, popping over the rim, Cian telling Sinead, 'Oh no, we've got one more pitch to do,' as a joke, and Sinead fighting back tears with a brave, 'OK, we'll have a drink and we'll get there,' only to whoop with crazy joy when I told her she'd made it, that this was the top.

Sending the two of them up to the tree, needing to know they were safe, I waited for Vanessa to appear, jugging a free-hanging rope from the belay after the bags were released. Again I sat in the dark and thought about what such an experience could do to a relationship. I joked it would either make or break us, but we were already made, so perhaps only had it all to lose. I wondered if I had betrayed myself here, used up that love in the fire of this thing. When I led or space-hauled the bags and she said, 'You make me hot,' did she mean it, or did I only show my Hyde self, uncompromising and heartless? I shouted into the night to see if she was safe.

And there she was too, jugging up, a pack on her back, stowing the rope as she went, looking as pro as any partner I'd had, experience forged in the doing. When she reached me, I think she was expecting a Hollywood embrace, but all she got was a quick kiss, neither of us free of the wall yet; the bags had to be hauled and we would not reach safe ground until midnight. It was late but no one seemed eager to get to bed, and so we sat around picking at the dregs of the food bags, drinking the rest of the red wine, listening to Nick Cave. Cian and Sinead looked like they were thankful for it to be over, so happy to feel solid ground again, to take off their harnesses and chuck them on the ground. I wondered how the climb would change them, especially Cian – if El Cap would change him like it once changed me. As for Vanessa, she looked like she was just sad not be on the wall any more, her ship ready to set sail again, her head full of walls, dreams we took with us as we drifted off to bed.

And so the following morning the two of us left our bivvy and slowly traipsed towards the top of El Cap, past trees ancient and thick with time, past boulders that seem carved by ancient climbers. The summit dome was under deep snow, and we walked hand in hand until there was no up left, only down all around. We stood and looked over towards Half Dome and waited.

I'd first climbed El Cap sometime in the 1990s with my friend Paul Tattersall, the two of us doing *The Shield*, both clueless really, ambition a steroid to experience. That climb was a life-changing event – El Cap had taken a place in my heart, had become a part of me. And I'd chosen well, because unlike most mountains, the Captain has never been a tormentor, only a mentor, silent but always teaching and pushing and demanding. Every moment of my life I feel its power running through me, its gift is a gift I have shared with as many people as I could, rewarded by seeing that change in them also. I have never asked anything of this rock but to let me pass, and it has given me so much more than I will ever truly understand. Without El Cap there would have been no Dru, no Troll, no Ulvetanna, no Vanessa. I am not a self-made man. I was made by this rock.

'Here comes the sun,' she said, my arms wrapped around her, the first flame of dawn lighting some far Sierra peak. We watched as the sun rose higher, felt its heat, aware that we were sharing a moment we'd not forget, all that effort worth it for this. Knowing there would never be a better time, I reached into my pocket and pulled out a small loop of three-millimetre cord cut from my camera case before we'd left the bivvy. It was a loop no wider than a woman's finger made thick by ten hard days on a big wall, tied with a fisherman's knot, the ends scraggy, but perfect still, perhaps the most important knot I would ever tie.

Bending down on one knee, I looked up at Vanessa, who looked down at me, thinking for a moment no doubt I was taking the piss, my Perlon ring in my hand, the question on my lips, no better time than now, no better woman, no better knot.

Bad Poetry: The Mountain

The Mountain does not love you.
Nor does it care
nor does it hate
or wish you harm
or wish you well.

The Mountain does not betray
trick, or beguile.
Say yes when it means no.
Act out of fear.
Act out of love.
Pull you in then throw you back
reject you
nor lead you astray,
or lead you home.

The Mountain does not dream
does not desire
does not want to fuck
or lay in your arms
make plans
have a life
or recollect
mull nor regret,
wake with tears in its eyes,
stop mid-sentence when one more word is one more too many.

It does not feel anything.

The Mountain cannot be saved by you
it dies slowly,
shattered and scarred by age,
feldspar, quartz, aragonite, calcite moving as swiftly as the stars – painlessly,
each grain washed away
and stone tumble
a lost heartbeat.
Yet unaware, vampire old, it does not feel nor fear death nor the time passing.

The Mountain has always been there, and always will
a lifetime together.
Your footsteps.
Your blood.
Your treasure.
Your sacrifice.
Unseen, unfelt, unknown.
But there is no history between it and you
no drama or recollection.
Good times or bad.
To be remembered in old age, or forgotten.
No memory of you
no sad wakings
or happy recollections.
You mean nothing.

The Mountain has no answers
no insight or revelation
no wisdom or stories
no path to take,
no kind words
or harsh.
But it will also never judge you,
never break you
nor do you harm
break your heart
or wish you unwell
nor plot
or scheme
or go crazy.

The Mountain offers you two gifts and that is all.

First the gift of certainty in all these things, that it will never change.
It neither loves nor hates, but only is.

The second is that all the things you may find upon its faces and walls and
couloirs and slopes, the love, wisdom, pain, longing, regret, friendship,
death, hope and humanity are not Mountain's gifts at all, but yours.

2
LOOKING ON

2.13

IMPERFECT BROTHER

I drive up through the Lake District's winding roads, sunny for a change, traffic shunting along in the usual dribs and drabs. I turn right up the hill and through the gates of the small house where tomorrow I'll be married. People are standing around the entrance, some having travelled a long way – only a small wedding if you're wondering where your invite went. As the car hits the gravel car park, I see a face more familiar than the rest, a face like mine, the way this man smiles, the way he stands, once smaller than me, but not so much now, now we are grown.

I'd not seen my brother Robin for years, and I mean years, our lives as separate as can be – as they often are – countries and worlds apart most of the time. Time. Only now, writing this, the idea just coming to me to write about him, do I see how far apart we are, how distant we've become – perhaps spending only a week together in total since our teens. How is that possible? And when we did see one another we most often stood behind our kids, cousins to each other, children like a garden wall, only gossip between us and not much more: weather chat, 'how are things going?', maybe the odd shared memory to make the kids laugh. We never talked about us, about the past, back then when we seemed as different as can be, the same cloth, only different sides. Time wears most cloth thin enough to see both faces. Brothers we may be, but how sad it is to think that blood can be so thin we should go almost thirty years like strangers.

Our grandma used to say that 'people have separate lives', and it's true, but that doesn't make it right, perhaps even makes it so – that saying a get-out-of-jail-free card, permission to see your blood as nothing more valuable or precious as running water. Once, you shared everything, grew up in the same bedroom, went to the same school, lived the same confined reality, and now the only thing you share is a glimpse through Facebook of what life is now.

To me, family seems to be like something you know is valuable, but that you put in a drawer, a safe place, and allow yourself to forget, forget that distraction, forget because you know its value is secure. You can love remotely and forever. Open the drawer and it's there. But when I go to Mass in Galway I am assailed by blood on the church steps, tripping and slipping over Vanessa's aunts and uncles, nieces and cousins, her family's house a gathering place where that blood is gossiped over, the shared past forever unpicked over tea. These people are not strangers to one other; they make time because they know time is fleeting. Never in my life have I been so surrounded by community and friendship and family as there, which only makes me see my shortcomings. I think about my sister Joanne, and her amazing daughter Lily who thinks I'm some Superman because I once lifted a settee up with one hand and tell a mean joke about wide-mouthed frogs. 'What's your other niece called?' asks Vanessa, seeing if I can finally remember the name of my sister's youngest child.

Thinking hard I say, 'Lily Number Two'. Vanessa rolls her eyes and asks why kids love me so much. 'Because I neglect them.'

Family, you take it for granted, of no importance to the twenty-first-century atomised human being, selfish as to its value. Yet now I have to ask: where have the years gone? I open the drawer and look inside and ask where are the drunken barbecues and family holidays, the stuff some take for granted, that time given to something so deserving? When did me and my baby brother sit down and reminisce; of that shared life, of my cruelty to him, him and his amazing 'rubber bones' that would not break? What would his story of me be and my story of him? 'Remember that time you tried to stab me with a knife?' should have been the whisky reminiscence, or 'remember that time I threw you into the docks?', but whenever we met it was never just us, like we were guilty of something, like our childhood was a trauma we could not talk about, or too far gone to be revisited or necessary. Looking back now, although we were very different, the only thing we shared was the urge to be gone – to leave and get on with life. Like a body sucked into an avalanche, trapped in the slide and taken along, we both fought hard not to become buried.

We took different paths, but both led up – steep and dangerous at times – and it's a marvel we ever came down. I remember that one time, the last time we met, a few weeks ago, at the wedding, the first time in years, him telling me about finding himself in a pitch-black Afghan night, in the middle of a minefield. This would be bad enough you'd imagine, but it was somewhat comical as he was inside a C-130 Hercules transport plane at the time, the pilot asking what they should do. He's told me bits of his life in the military, and I mean his *life*, from a kid posted to Northern Ireland to now, a troubleshooter, working out how to get shit done, my brother a spreadsheet warrior these days. Maybe it's a blood thing, but I feel the toll those wars have taken on his life, the burden of others, never for Queen or Country, but for another kind of blood, people you cannot so easily neglect. I often get a whiff of something when you tell someone your brother's in the military, that some caste system operates in polite society, that he's lower than us, that he's part of the problem – like Trident, that if retired would make the world a better place. But Robin has been beyond the city walls; he knows why the world needs people like him, who give so much but get so little back, no pension recompense, real 'heroes', not just people with dangerous 'jobs'. When I look at his sense of duty to others – to all of us in a way – I think about that line some now-dead soldier once wrote: 'If not me, then who else?' My brother has done more good in this world than anyone I have ever met, and maybe he makes me feel my own life has been nothing but selfish and childish. But on the rare occasions when we met the strain was too much to look at; in his eyes, the way he buzzed like a dodgy appliance about to burst into flames or just stop dead. Maybe that's why we never saw each other, not through a lack of love, but because it was too painful to see. What people say about you behind your back is the real mark of a man, and I've met many individuals who served with my brother, KP, and they only ever said good things; through the bad times, the coffin days, and the good, when he stopped bringing the coffins back.

He is younger than me, my baby brother, but he has grey hair while mine is still black.

I invite him to my wedding, and he tells me he'll try and come, a man who can never stray far from a job that is beyond overstretched, some trouble always brewing in the world. Part of me doesn't mind if he comes or not, after all, I never see him anyway. He's in the drawer, safe. I also don't want this to be a burden on him. But there he is, he's made it, standing in the gravel as we pull up, my future wife who he's never met beside me, his kids almost all grown up like mine, walls still between us. Kids aren't kids for long, it's true, but neither are we. There he is my baby brother, old rubber bones, thick and dependable and robust, someone who I could call up in the middle of the night and know he'd come, something I guess he's made a career out of – dependability, one of life's most overlooked commodities.

And so we stand in the car park, awkward at first, a little shy, both complicit to how things are, how things will always be. But then we hug, and it's like hugging myself. He squeezes me hard, and I squeeze him back, these boys, these brothers, all grown. I hug this man, more like me than anyone else who will ever live, and also just as imperfect, but blood all the same.

2.14

A CRYING GIRL

Tears roll down her face as I write about things of no real importance, her one table away, this girl crying. She is sitting opposite her boyfriend, white cups held tight in their hands, held tight for an hour as the seaside drizzle mists the window beside them. They hold on to their cups for some hard comfort, comfort for hands that would once have held each other.

His body is rugby large, grey fluffy fleece, but young, an Irish butcher's boy, head shaven, but with a face soft, and soft for her, even in this moment of hardness. He is young enough perhaps for this to be new to him, but maybe not, a young man not often so firm when tears oppose that certainty. It takes a lot to stand firm against the sobs of someone you once loved, that conversation that winds from despair, shame and destitution, to the strength to look aloof from it all, a little anger – but more to come – maybe even a story to show how 'good we were'. But those sad sparkling eyes soon go, she wants him to stay, sends out one hand for his, then pulls it back and shakes in her seat. She is not too proud to beg, something easy to write, but which makes me wonder how many reading this know what it does, such a thing.

If not forever how about just now. She wants him to come round, to her, on the couch where she sits, and hug this thing away. But he knows it is a trap. Her drink is full; his is empty.

A few days ago I sat somewhere else and saw another girl cry, her boyfriend sitting opposite her, the whole time on his phone, tapping away as she looked down at her plate. My writer's mind wondered what their story was, that a simple reading never reveals the truth; that instead of being an asshole, he did not ignore her because he didn't love her, but because he wanted her to no longer love him. Tears have an amazing effect on people though, they snap you back, flow without stopping at the rational mind, go straight to the heart. And so he put down his phone and asked 'what's wrong?', when he knew full well.

If I was some alien sitting there with my coffee, looking out from the corners of my eyes, I'd marvel at these human beings, their drama, how odd they act, against their better interest, so damaged and damaging to each other, lashing out and dragging at the world for someone to hold them near. I thought about Joan Crawford, one of the most intelligent and desirable film stars of her age, saying after getting her Oscar in 1946 that it would be the only man who'd never leave her. If I'd been an alien it would have been easy, like seeing two monkeys fighting, but I'm not; I just wanted him to leave so I could say what people always say: 'You're too good for him.'

The girl near me has stopped crying; she's strong, smiling as if at love that's new, not love that's dying. I think of that saying, 'nothing dries faster than tears', but as I begin to wonder why that is – something to do with salt – she grabs her elbows, her face goes red, and she begins to cry again, the boyfriend sitting back, hard. 'I used to have fantasies that he'd die,' I hear in my head, from a woman I once knew, admitting that someone's death would be easier than this. Neat and tidy, not like this grisly murder.

The boyfriend fiddles with his keys and she cries again, her hands so eager to reach out, to at least be friends – the rope the desperate cling to for as long as they can, perhaps one way to pull them back. I imagine how she sees him in her mind – bear-like, soft and warm, the smell of his fleece, his hair, his butcher's-boy skin.

He stands, she puts on her coat, the drizzle outside now rain. I wonder how it's possible to look on upon such a drama – the drama that is all around us – without any feeling. Then I see the pink marshmallows floating in her now-cold hot chocolate, untouched but for her tears, and I feel like crying too.

2.15

CHONGO BY THE POWER

'I wake each morning filled with hate,' said Chongo as I stood to leave the table, a wincing self-indictment, the punchline to the 'stupidity' and 'obedience' of his fellow Americans sitting at tables all around us in the Yosemite Valley Lodge cafeteria, shovelling in their pancakes before hitting the trail. I laughed like it was a joke, or if not a joke then so that in laughing I'd take some of the edge off such a man as this being filled with such nasty sentiment. But Chongo didn't parry my smile with another, his wrinkled face remained uncracked. Instead, I got a slow nod. 'Filled with hate.'

Our long conversation that morning had begun around eight with *Vogue*'s war photographer Lee Miller in Hitler's bath, and ended about ten via a winding trail with the Jesuits, Chongo unpicking their vows of chastity, poverty and obedience as a metaphor for American society. The only interruptions had come from people wanting to use the power socket by our feet, the only one in the cafeteria that worked, the search for power the anxiety of our age.

Chongo was the first and only homeless big-walling quantum mechanic I'd ever met, a man I first bumped into living in the trees below *Tangerine Trip* at the base of El Cap in 1997. Seeing his things hanging in a tree I'd been told by another climber, 'Oh those are Chongo's', conjuring up an image of some monster Vietnam vet living wild, faded army fatigues cut off at the knees and shoulders, a climbing Tasmanian devil. But the man himself, when he appeared a few days later as I belayed Paul Tattersall on the first pitch of *Zenyatta Mondatta*, a route far less cool once you realise it's named after a Police album, is no Tasmanian, yet he did not disappoint – a devil of another form.

'If you want to be bitchin' you need to look bitchin',' said Chongo, touting a bottle of tequila, toasting the walls, the sun only just painting the boulder where I sat. 'Do you smoke?' he asked, and I didn't, which was a shame, as to get stoned with such a man is what dope was made for. 'Everything you need falls from these walls,' said Chongo, as Paul shouted down for me to focus on his A4 lead, not some hobo-alco bullshit. 'You just wish for it, and it falls from the walls,' he added, a light tinkle coming as a full stop to the sentence as a wire landed about a hundred metres away, dropped by a team on *The Shortest Straw*. 'See,' he said, hobbling and stumbling over the talus to snaffle it up. 'Dude! Number one BD Stopper!' Chongo shouted, slipping it into his holey, tatty shorts, where it fell out on to the floor again unseen. Turning around, he declared, 'Fuck, and here's another one!'

That memory came back to me as I stood to leave, Chongo's hate hanging in the space between us above the empty plates and saucers. Not the whole memory, but the essence of this man, this stealthy legend, like it betrayed him as not the man I'd wanted him to be, but as the man I'd always been afraid he was – and whom most others only ever saw.

Chongo's words often stick like that, stay around in your head, in the heads of better men than me as well if you'd imagine me easy prey to a well-turned idea. His ideas can change the shape of your thoughts a little, sometimes a lot: the light tickle of an idea, or like a mad dog zipped inside a bouncy castle. Like the time on a big wall or any good climb, you come away changed – well, the hard ones. I remember reading his *The Homeless Interpretation of Quantum Mechanics on the Reticent Wall* in 2001, some line about past, present and future only being an illusion, or how matter cannot be killed, only changed from one state to another, that nothing dies – ideas that come around like a cheque in the post when you're on the bones of your arse. Other memories are less intense, like showing me how to get free food, explaining that children always ask parents for five pancakes but only ever eat one. Now, like I always see Dean Potter in the wing of any raven that passes by while on the wall, I always see Chongo in the hungry eyes of any child queuing for food at the lodge.

And so I think Chongo is a man worth taking the time to listen to, that he adds value to those who can listen – which is a skill – and not just wait their turn to speak. He makes you laugh; he makes you think. He's a man whose wisdom often goes unheard. You see it when you know him, sit beside or near him in that cafeteria, how he's almost invisible to most, how the clean world, the world without holes, the world that smells nice as you pass it on the trail, can't see him at all. Chongo is a man who could easily creep unseen into the dragon's lair to steal its treasure ... well, if that dragon wore creased chino shorts and an Under Armour vest. Chongo wears a disguise you see – well you don't see, my point really – few recognising that his vagrant sun-dark skin and flophouse threads are not the uniform of a homeless man, but the stoic shamanic robes of his very majesty. They are not the American Dream most people imagine, raised suspension and garage full of junk; their reality is a delusion. But Chongo, his reality is as old as the walls around us. He is Yosemite, not them; he knows this place and its nature greater than any ranger, mere tourists to nature. He and John Muir would get on like a house on fire, far more than Muir and a park administrator. You cannot know the wild nature of the world when you sleep in a bed, you can't see it on a bank statement, only know plaster over your head instead of stars, not know how a bear thinks until you too have sung for your supper, your head stuck in a trash can. Poverty makes you wiser than any king.

Chongo's ability to cloak himself is how The Man had so much trouble surveilling him all those years while he lived in the park illegally. It's a skill you find in many places in nature; people who turn down your beds in fancy hotels, the Loch Ness monster, baby pigeons. But if you can see this man on his parallel plane, take the time to respond and listen to this man who flies at wave height, ask an opening question such as 'So, you like math?' or, 'I'm guessing you're educated,' as he goes table to table, it's worth seeing him blip on your radar.

But, of course, Chongo is not invisible. We choose not to see such people, and I admit that morning I'd almost done the same, pretended not to see him sitting there.

I'd not seen Chongo for a good ten years following his banishment from the Valley, so it was strange seeing him back after so long, on his throne in the cafeteria; all his worldly possessions in his tired-looking backpack next to the toilet door, the saddlebags of a long life on the road. He was sitting alone, looking a little lost, the canteen empty still, the sun yet to peek up from behind the range of light, sitting beside the only plugs that worked, where the climbers always gathered like moths.

And now for a confession to this old friend: for a moment I hesitated with my tray, not immediately sitting down beside him as I had countless times. I hesitated, even though here was a man who could recall my name, a man with whom I shared some history. Why? The obvious answer would be Chongo is a man somehow contaminated, infected, tainted, some stink to him you can't smell, but one that most steer clear of, a component to his invisibility. Part madness, part poverty, part the leprosy we most often just walk past, the leper at your feet proffering an empty cup for your change, looking for pity. But Chongo only ever gives, not looking for small change, the currency he seeks just ears and ideas, to simply give him

107

some time, which is maybe worse, his ideas and thoughts close enough to some visionary truth to be madness. My reason for hesitating was different, after all only the insane or lost ever really speak the truth. I hesitated because I saw Chongo sitting there like a man at the last supper, only one ten years' stale; so surrounded by its ghosts, the dead, the departed and the elsewhere. What I saw in Chongo was what I saw in myself, that like me he was lost a little in time, yesterday another country, yesterday another place he'd been thrown out of. You see Yosemite is a place where memories are richer than in almost any other, a rich mix of passion and joy, fear and endeavour, the walls around us places where life's greatest moments are often beat out. Here at these tables lifelong friendships are made, ones that last a single serving yet sustain. When I sit here I cannot help but think of those people I've shared so many mornings, afternoons and nights with, talking from opening to closing, a dirtbag youth club. I think of Leo, the Hubers, Timmy O'Neill, Pep, Tommy and Beth, Alex Honnold and Dean Potter, and so many partners and friends, the buzz, the shared stories and dreams, epics and great escapes. These were the greatest days of our lives, and here was where we came down, where we decompressed and debriefed, at these very tables. This place is more than tables and medium-quality junk food and stolen coffee. And so we run back here, to feel such feelings again, back to the fellowship of this space, to sit and plan, scribble out topos and get the beta, and to return with tales of what we took, what it took, and what remained. But Yosemite, this place that remains unchanged, is forever changing, always moving on, stones falling in the dark. To allow the spell of yesterday to be cast on you here is to be eroded by the sadness of a valley both changing and unchanged, for it to be like the first time, yet always haunted by the ghosts of seasons past. How could a surfer find his greatest wave if he stood on the shore mourning his last?

I feel this, this little mourning for the past, and I wonder if ultimately that's why those who love this place so much eventually choose to stay away.

I hesitated, saw my loss in his, but steeled myself and went to sit with this great man.

'I'm full of hate,' he repeated. 'Really,' he added, maybe seeing my surprise. 'Filled with it.' I laughed again, because I was uncomfortable, maybe to persuade this man so full of honesty, hard-won wisdom and raw humanity that he was wrong about that, after all, it's easy to misdiagnose such a feeling; love, despair or longing can feel just the same – that hate can be a misdiagnosis of something good, you can feel as sick with love as with a belly full of E. coli. I laughed, but he was gone, and so I walked away.

I try not to judge anyone these days, still, it was like Bill Murray admitting to such a thing, but then would I feel anything but hate if I lay my homeless head down on some Santa Cruz street each night only to wake homeless again in the morning? Who was I to judge such a man, his cruel reality simply bisecting mine in that narrowest of meetings, both tourists to each other?

As I stepped out of the door, down the stairs past people waiting for the bus to Merced, I wondered if, like me, Chongo had realised long ago, an old hand to a transitory world, that you could only return here if you embraced now and tomorrow, not then and yesterday. He is a hunter-gatherer of the greatest skill, searching not just for the grubs and roots of the cafeteria leftovers, but for the rich picking of time spent sharing stories and ideas with fellow travellers as sustaining as a child whose eyes are bigger than their belly's breakfast.

Passing by the window, squirrels darting amongst the picnic tables in search of crumbs, I looked in at him one last time, silent, stone-like, brave in this new world. I saw his face flicker and light up, but not for this stale dinner, but as a bunch of fresh young climbers, Adam Ondra amongst them, sat down around him, holding out hands to shake to this invisible man, guardian and gatekeeper, sitting on his throne, rich as any king, where he knew the moths fluttered close, canny as ever, like any great forager, by the power.

As it happens, just as words open doors, so do blogs; within an hour of writing this I had an email from the man himself, saying that I had talent but had missed the nature of his hate, not simple hate, but a hatred of 'traditions of ignorance'. Amen to that.

2.16

LONG RUNS THE FOX

I first met Ricky Bell in the dust of Camp 4. I forget the year. Ricky is one of those people you meet in life: one minute unknown, the next never to be forgotten. I've met a lot of 'legends': some who weren't and knew it groaned beneath their untruth; others who were – the best – and didn't even know it. It's a testament to Ricky that 'I know Ricky' is the reply of anyone who's ever met him – never 'I once met him'. It's rare to hear 'I've heard of him'. No one's heard of Ricky Bell, *the* Ricky Bell, and yet they should have. Here lies part of the charm of the man.

And so on that day, one minute there was a space at the picnic table at Camp 4, my site next to the disabled toilets – I remember that – the next, there was Ricky Bell. He looked like some Irish Dickensian waif, chalk dust and dust on his clothes, which I also remember were a bit ragged, seams chewed by gnawing cracks. His clothes were devoid of the badges of talent most great climbers tend to wear, which they need to bolster that self-belief that they're a pro. Instead, he looked like he'd ram-raided a charity shop. Again, part of his charm.

Before his clothes there were his sparkly eyes and a wicked grin – a smile, maybe a smirk, that on some dark street would make you check your pockets, worried he was on some Fagin's errand. The funny thing about Ricky is that his smile always makes me think he knows something I don't, but not in a smug way. It was only while writing this that I finally understood where that smile comes from – I've only ever met him when he's climbing.

Like many young Turks you meet in Camp 4, Ricky was testing himself: Half Dome in a day, *The Nose* in a day, *Astroman*, the Rostrum, a proud ticklist. You could feel his passion for climbing – his passion to live – shake the table as we sat and talked. You meet a lot of hotshots in Yosemite; some go on to greatness, but most get bogged down in the sticky stuff of living. Few sustain the high pitch of their youthful ambition and keep shaking. Ricky did.

A long time later – last year maybe, I forget – I was standing in a dark Dublin car park, outside the climbing wall where Ricky often sets routes. Ricky was showing me his van, his house and home, probably all he owned beyond his gear. He looked the same as he had when I first met him, still dusty with chalk, clothes still nibbled, still that smile as he slid open the side door to show a bedroom dank and cramped, full of tools, climbing gear and more chalk dust. It was a bivvy, not a bed. He looked the same as when I'd first met him, but now he was a master, perhaps one of the best trad climbers in the world, his routes unreported, undergraded. Ask them though, the stars, to name someone who stands out in this risky business, a bold life and boltless death, and I'm sure Ricky would feature. I stuck my head inside his home and thought it so strange a man with so much talent would choose this over something a little richer – maybe even just a bigger van, or perhaps just a tidier one. I began a familiar talking-to that I give men and women of great talent, but who put passion before bread and butter, that they are missing the trick, that they need to play the game – maybe not the whole game, but some part of it. Ricky smiled, as usual, probably eager to get back to the wall, yet happy to listen, but no doubt well aware of the hoops of success.

'Nah,' he said. 'I just go climbing.'

Now I know it sounds like I fell in love with Ricky at that moment in Camp 4, and yes, I probably did, but then everyone falls in love with Ricky Bell – people who have those rarest of charms. Ricky is a role model for me, a man who has what most of us wish we had, yet don't have the guts to take: not fame or success or acknowledgement for his mastery, but the guts to take nothing at all, and so never compromise what his life is all about.

3
GEAR AND TECHNIQUE

3.17

LIFE AT RETAIL

'I'm going to leave a nut,' I said, crouching down, tugging at the rotten rap slings jammed beneath a couch-sized boulder. 'I don't trust these slings.'

'What?! We've lost two nuts already,' said Vanessa. 'I'm sure it'll be grand, those Italians rapped off it earlier.'

I looked again at the anchor: faded, chewed up by ropes and rodents, short loops tied around long loops, the usual dangerous jazz of a bad rap anchor, illogical, the same old mania that climbers create when they just want off. I ran my fingers around the slings, felt the wear and the damage. Was I a wimp? I looked down to the ground, the sixty-metre ropes only just touching the snow patch at the base, imagined that awful freefall if the anchor pulled, imagined those final thoughts.

It had been a long day on *Lucky Streaks*, a classic Tuolumne 5.10 on Fairview Dome, and our feet were in bits, weakening our resolve for the last 'easy' 5.8 pitch and so instigating a descent back down the route. So far we'd only left gear we'd found on other routes, and two nuts and two krabs, the traversing nature of the route necessitating placing gear by the first one down in order to hit each belay. Although we were retreating, it also seemed like a good lesson in how to get off traversing routes, how to set up safe rap anchors, and how to handle ropes on such ground so they don't get stuck. And now we were at the last belay, the end in sight. 'It'll be grand,' repeated Vanessa, just wanting level ground.

Although as a climber I don't seem to have progressed much since the age of sixteen with regard to technical difficulty, one thing I've become an expert on is abseil anchors. I've seen them all: lovely safe bolted anchors that could hold an elephant, ice threads, dodgy spikes, retrievable ice screws, a tied-off knifeblade in only one inch, snow bollards. I've also become well acquainted with fixed stuff that breaks – slings and cord – and know it just goes BANG! No creaking. No warning. The worst is tape, which can look in good condition, but with one little bad patch, plus serious sun damage, it will just rip apart like paper. Cord is better, the sheath soaking up the rays, but even then a seven-millimetre strand of cordelette abandoned on a flake several years before you arrive is a dice-rolling anchor. What about when you put all the junk together, as was the case on Fairview Dome, several strands of crap, all threaded through two rap rings? Yes, there is strength in numbers, and I'll never forget the rap anchor on the *American Direct* on the Dru – some spike that must have had thirty loops of tape and cord around it. Thinking logically, if each piece was only able to hold twenty kilograms then together they would be OK. And then there were the three Italians who had rapped off while we'd been there. But they were Italians, who like most continentals have a crazy trust in fixed junk. I've seen French climbers belay off a single old fixed peg, no testing, just clip and hang, bringing up two partners, all done with bomber cracks all around. Maybe I am a wimp, maybe this attitude is why Brits are so slow, but maybe this is why Brits – unused to fixed anchors on mountain crags – don't die when belays rip out on alpine climbs.

One of the most revealing stories along these lines was Roger Mear's descent from some route in the Écrins. Following two Spanish climbers down a steep wall, he arrived at a rap anchor comprising of one Lost Arrow, with both Spaniards hanging from it. Roger, being tough enough not to care what others thought of him, thought the anchor dicey, and so slipped in a nut and quickdraw, clipping this into the peg's krab. The second the gate shut – BANG! – the peg pulled, both Spanish climbers falling on to Roger's wire.

I looked at the slings again, measuring up what I knew about slings and cords, breaking strains, the cost of leaving a nut, cursing myself for not having any cord to just add my own piece to the junk show. I looked up at Vanessa – my wife – and thought about her mum, crying as we left Galway, me telling her I'd keep her daughter safe.

'I'm placing a nut as a backup,' I said, sticking in a Wild Country Superlight 10 under the boulder and using my prusik loop to tie it into the rap rings. Then I set up an anchor with two cams to act as a backup to the main anchor and which Vanessa would take out once I'd gone down (I weigh 100 kilograms while Vanessa weighs sixty).

Set up, I threaded the ropes. 'I'll bring that nut down with me,' Vanessa said, half joking. I gave her a serious look, then told her the story of two climbers who'd been descending the Midi. One had put a new Dyneema sling on to a spike full of crappy slings, to the protest of his partner, who said everyone used these slings. But the first climber would not be dissuaded, even if he seemed a wimp. Safe on the sling he rapped to the bottom of the route and shouted 'off'. A minute later his partner began down, then without warning his friend was freefalling, crashing down the wall in a mess of rope until he struck the base, dead. Around his neck was the Dyneema sling.

Ten minutes later we were both on the ground, safe and sound.

'I'm sure that anchor was grand,' repeated Vanessa. But therein lies the rub of such paranoia, the cost of which when you're wrong is death, the cost of not finding out around £9.

3.18

A MILE FURTHER DOWN THE ROAD

When someone dies somewhere cold or steep my phone starts ringing and my inbox fills up with messages, pinging in from radio, TV and the papers, wanting an opinion on the tragedy of someone else's adventure. I tend not to respond any more, as I eventually asked myself the question: for whose benefit would I reply? Would it be mine? Out of hubris, to be supportive or critical or nonplussed, humping some small jizz of fame out of the dead. Would it be to help sell papers, fill in some broadcast time; just a voice to link another story, filler between Islamist terror and economics? Or would it be to put forward a defence for the dead? And, if so, why bother? People will either understand anyway or a sentence or two will never do justice to someone's tragedy.

I'll admit when I do answer the phone – a rarity, in fact I don't really have a mobile phone any more, just a phone I use in the UK that sits in a drawer here in Ireland – and a nice man or woman asks me a question, I can't help myself but to give an opinion. I always try and be as heartless and detached as possible, leaving it for others to add the snowflakes – I'd ask no less from any of my mates ... but please, *please*, don't allow my life to be summed up by a cheesy line from Bear Grylls.

In early 2016 my phone and inbox came alive following the passing of Henry Worsley, who had died of bacterial peritonitis no doubt caused by pushing his body over 913 miles of Antarctic ice with the aim of being the first to cross the continent alone, without kites and without support. It came as a shock having only seen the news on explorersweb.com the day before that he'd made the decision to pull the plug on his expedition after seventy-one days – I've been trying to get funding for a trip like this for years, so I know once you're there you're going to kill yourself before you fail. I actually began writing something about his death, about the nature of men and women that have been successful in their overreaching, how maybe instead of one torture after another, one should realise that things are placed beyond the grasp of the human body for a reason. But what did I know about Henry's death to comment?

His death did make me think about how hard I've pushed my body and mind in the past, making the assumption I could take it all. If you look at the photo of me back in the Valley after my fourteen-day solo of *Sea of Dreams*, it's pretty shocking – maybe the best image I've got to illustrate the physical cost one pays.

What you don't see is that my haulbags were still hanging on the last pitch, left there because I was too exhausted to haul them up, that after only one day off I had to hike back to the top to haul them up and carry them down, one at a time, leaving at 4 a.m. to get the last bag the day I had to leave. Twice on the way to the airport I had to stop and sleep, only to wake from a nightmare that I was actually a) asleep while driving, or b) still on the wall. At the time a few people asked, 'Why don't you just pay someone to carry them down for you?', which walking up in the dark with legs as stiff as boards seemed like a good idea – you only meet BASE jumpers at that time of the morning – but one I rejected, after all this was a test: to pay someone would be to fail.

My piece on training 'D.F.Y.U' – Don't Fuck Yourself Up – gets quite a lot of hits online and maybe I should write one for the body and mind combined as it's easy to forget you are a finely balanced organic machine, not one of the X-Men. There are negative long-term problems if you imagine yourself a machine or superhuman. It's fine for others to think so, but most heroes are made weaker by their own worship. I focus on being shit and lazy and slow in just about everything. I've never been a proponent of the phrase 'Work hard, play hard', instead going for my alternative, if less healthy or Protestant: 'Make play work, eat cake.'

I once met a mate of a guy who'd broken the record for cycling Land's End to John o' Groats, riding non-stop for two and a bit days, his time something stupid like fifty hours. I remember this conversation because this man described how his mate the cyclist, the fittest guy he knew, was never the same again, that his record had cost him some part of his life force. I've heard this said by others, people who've given it all, their bodies and minds falling apart as soon as they reached their goal, some never making it back to 100 per cent. Pete Whittaker described this post-objective breakdown following his ascent of *Century Crack*, the culmination of two years of intensive training, which left him ill and fatigued as soon as his objective was reached.

I had a mate who'd been in the SAS – the proper SAS. He told me that at the end of the SAS selection exercise, a process designed to wear you to the nub, you have to do a huge solo march. You're on your own, carrying a twenty-five-kilogram rucksack and rifle while navigating and marching through the night. He told me how you have to dig deeper than you thought you ever could, into your muscles, into your mind. At the end the few that make it arrive at a checkpoint with not one gram of anything left to give. They're told, 'Right, the lorry home is one mile down the road, if you miss it you're off'. Tired bodies stand and push on, beyond themselves, just bloody and raw and hungry for it to be done. And there it is, after a crucifying mile, its tailgate open, tea urn steaming, the last thirty metres almost worth the mile it took to get there. But the lorry moves on before they get there, around a bend. 'One more mile!' an instructor shouts, at which point minds and bodies snap and will not move. The few that can shuffle on, around the corner, and not far beyond – the truck waiting for them for real.

This ability to keep going is maybe what sets some apart from others, although I've had few that could not keep up – and the few that didn't were the last I'd ever suspect. One of the most fucked people I ever climbed with was Major Phil Packer, a man who's grasped the pain of doing in order to mask the pain of being. When we climbed El Cap he had never climbed anything before, and ended up doing 4,000 pull-ups to make it to the top. He never told me his Headley Court doctors had told him to do no more than three hours' exercise a day, or that he was on morphine, and so on his first day he climbed for about twenty-two hours, the whole time in terrible pain. I knew we had to keep going to a good ledge, important if one of the team can't walk, so kept pushing him until he was one pitch below the ledge at about 3 a.m. By now he was beyond knackered, falling in and out of consciousness, the whole team shattered. Seeing it was beyond him to climb the last forty metres, I shouted up, 'Send down a rope for Phil, I think he needs a pull up this last bit'. Phil, suddenly awake, replied, 'Fuck that,' and somehow found the energy to jug up.

I can only speculate what happened to Henry, his death perhaps caused by overall crushing fatigue or a single injury magnified by the unrelenting pressure. Very often you can start a trip feeling more alive than you ever have before, yet by the end know in your flaccid heart how easy it would be to simply drop dead. I never understood the phrase 'died of exhaustion' until I first felt close to it.

So what is this, a eulogy to Henry or an explanation? Well it's neither, more of a heads-up to anyone who wishes to fill Henry's shoes, or anyone else they admire, because very often it's nothing to do with brains, good looks, sponsorship, what kit you've got, but the simple ability to keep going, inch after inch, mile after mile, month after month. Your training should reflect that: days on the hill, long, long days, where the end always seems – and maybe always and forever will be – a mile further down the road.

Bad Poetry: Winter

The beginning and the end.

Waiting. Dreaming. Making plans. Buying new picks or resharpening the old. The first snow. Excitement that makes you feel like a child again. Early morning alarms. Warm beds you have to leave. Skidding a car that's not yours to skid. Cold so deep there's no smell. Feeling unfit on long dark approaches. Cursing the snow you've waited so long for. Feeling the sun and appreciating a warmth so subtle perhaps it isn't even there. Ill-fitting boots. Toenails you meant to cut. Stepping through ice into unseen streams as you curse your misfortune. Partners' laughter. Joining in. Scary snow slopes you know you shouldn't cross – but do. Head-pounding, lung-ripping, leg-screaming fear. Avalanches that turn out to be jumbo jets on the way to the Caribbean. Fancy new crampons and ripped gaiters. More curses and more laughter. Racking up – feeling your heart beat with apprehension within your layers. The snap of the crampon binding. The tightening bind of the wrist loop. The first lead of the year. Feeling the vibration run up your arm as you twang home the first pick. Cursing gummy cams, and krabs that stick to your fingers – wires that burn your tongue. Picks through new ropes. Committing yourself. Getting steep. Fumbled screws that will never be found. Bloodied knuckles and bruised toes. Cursing those knocking down ice from above – beyond caring about those below. Farmyard noises that come unexpectedly to your lips. Ice screws that always seem too far below. Hollow ice. Fragile ice. Trying to rest – only to waste more energy trying. Pushing into the red. Going for broke. Flogging a dead horse. Running on empty. Hands that can't grip – but have to – and will. Praying for a top rope. Believing that it can't get any worse. Spindrift in your face. Losing it big style. Whimpering. Beyond reason. The best pitch of your life. Reaching the top. Screaming out loud. Wanting to cry – but holding it back. Wanting to laugh – and laughing like crazy. Sitting all alone and happy to be that way – listening to the growing silence of a slowly fading heartbeat. It's snowing hard and you never even noticed. Your partner shouting 'tight!' – about to come off. One eye on the belay praying they won't. Your partner screaming as they come off. Straining legs to save the belay. A panting friend coming into view. Tired smiles and shaking hands – and heads – and bodies. A storm that hits without you even noticing. Lips so cold they can't form words. Broken goggles that were rubbish anyway. Getting lost. The long arguing descent. A death march out. Hunger. Cold. Dark. Longer than you thought. Tired mind playing tricks. Napoleon's soldiers staggering with you across the Russian steppe. Car headlights on the highway. George Bailey running down the road shouting 'Merry Christmas!' The scrape of boots on gravel. Sitting in the car with the heater on full – just sitting. The end of a day of photos untaken but memories that will never thaw. Home. Skidding again. Big meals. Tall stories. Mulled wine spilt on white carpets. Cold feet and hot bodies in bed. The beginning of a season of falling in love with ice – often unrequited, and falling out of love – but not for long. Dreaming of warm stone. Waiting.

The end and the beginning.

4
LIFE, DEATH AND IN BETWEEN

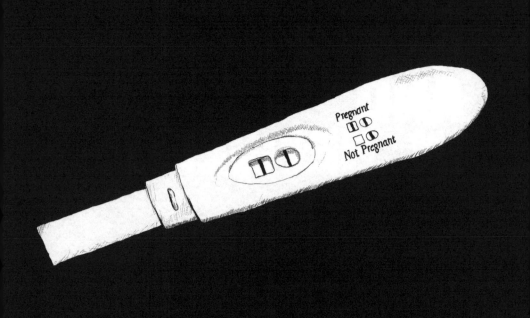

4.19

THE HAUNTED CLIFF

I have a friend who tells the story of a haunted cliff.

He and his wife were kayaking to Greenland from Ellesmere Island. They hopped along the coast until they could make the sea crossing between the land and the ice, dodging polar bears and walruses that could suck out their intestines. One evening they came to a great camping spot below a high cliff. They pulled up their boats and set about making camp, that long weary slog of tent poles and stuff sacks, boats made safe against Arctic winds that can rise at any moment. When they had settled down, the stove purring away, my friend's wife said she didn't like this place, that something was wrong. My friend laughed this off as nothing more than a mind as sore as its body, that same unease that has you hearing polar bears behind you as you wash up at the water's edge. But she said 'no'; there was something wrong with this place. She stood and packed, no discussion at all, she was leaving, they were both leaving. They packed their boats and paddled on into the Arctic twilight.

The Inuit don't believe someone has a soul until they are given a name, the name being the soul and reincarnation. Inuit names are genderless and passed on from the dead to the living – of any sex. All Inuit are sexless by name until they reach adulthood – the name of an uncle, drowned at sea, can be passed down to his sister's baby girl. The named spirit leaves the grave and finds the baby within the womb.

The Inuit, like many cultures that once lived close to the edge, had no use for sentimentality. Babies were once traded, given away or discarded, depending on the need or the want of the group, while we in the West would choose to save our children over ourselves or die together. For the Inuit, the masters of survival, the continuation of the line was all that mattered, that the soul name should be known and live on.

When I moved to Ireland, for the first time in my life I came face to face with people opposed to abortion. For my liberal Western mind, the idea of opposition was extreme; this was something unquestionable, a human right. I saw such people as dangerous and radical, like members of the Ku Klux Klan, their views making me wary of them, their flawed thinking there for all to see. These people went on marches, stood and collected money for the cause, even laid down their lives to save lives. I saw them as crazy of course, indoctrinated and brainwashed by the Catholic Church, that cynical and patronising way of seeing the world when your own views are armed by total conviction. I think in civilised British society such people would be so marginalised you'd never come across them, apart from little groups standing with their signs behind barriers in town, the odd spokesperson or talking head, nutcases, God botherers. But here in Ireland, such people are not extremists. Abortion is still illegal, and those in need of it go over the border to the north, or to the UK mainland.

My liberal view was that I had known many people who'd had abortions, and none had done so without bearing the most terrible weight, and worse still they had carried a terrible guilt. It was no easy thing. But they knew I had no need to explain it. These fighters were not inhuman, uncaring, unthinking of the consequences of what they defended, but the total opposite. The arguments were mostly the same, like two men arguing backwards and forwards between a chasm neither could cross. Just making noise. But I'm a man who tries more and more to loosen my grip on the baggage of certainty, to want to jump that chasm, to make an ally of my opponent's truth. I began to see how such arguments were often framed, how within a second of debating what could easily be seen as some small murder of your own child, a serious moral question far from easy or binary, things were escalated to: 'What if someone's been raped?' You see this all the time, how a simple argument of how climbing isn't full of misogyny gets the response, 'Well, you've never been sexually assaulted'. The truth lies within a trap on a hair trigger. Once upon a time, I'd have stayed clear of such things, having no need of what lay within, but less so these days. In those conversations, late at night, I did what a man needs to do if they want to understand; not just listen to their own well-rehearsed truth, but to everyone's.

A universal truth that's easy to ignore in times like these is that every single person is fully justified to believe they are right. No one deserves to be treated as if their reality is any less valid to them than our own without taking the time to understand just what they think.

And then one day, sitting with some friends, one of them burst into tears, the story coming out that she was pregnant. The baby, like most babies, was not coming at the right time – unplanned and out of the blue;

the relationship one that was still growing. People around me looked excited for her, the Irish ones for babies, and told her it would be OK as the tears rolled down her cheeks. I didn't smile, I knew the strain a baby could bring too early in a relationship, when the joints of two lives were still to be set hard. I didn't smile, but instead, thinking I would be the voice of reason, of pragmatism, said, 'There are other options'. Just like that, as easy as can be. They all turned and looked at me, confused at what I'd said, confused at what I could be saying, about this amazing woman and the amazing baby she would have. And in that instant, I realised I was not the sane one, but the radical, murderous of some inopportune miracle. I was lost for words, shocked that such an idea could come as easily as that.

As for the haunted cliff.

My friend and his wife paddled on until they arrived at a small Inuit village. They pulled up their boats and crashed out, all thoughts of the haunted cliff forgotten. But in the morning an old woman came over to see how they were, her skin wrinkled by a life in the far north, an old woman who once upon a time, when her teeth were so worn she could not soften seal skin, would have been sent out into the night. She asked where they had come from, and they told her of their long and tough journey along the most barren of coasts.

'Did you stay below the big cliffs?' she asked.

They knew at once where she meant. 'For a short while,' they both replied.

'Did you hear the babies?' she asked, mournfully. 'That is where we threw them when we had no food to feed them.'

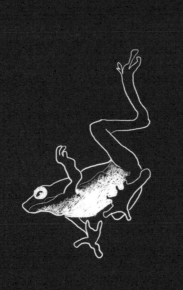

4.20

A PIECE OF WOOD

There is a block of wood at the end of my bed; four inches square, an inch thick, wrapped in the rubber of a car inner tube. This piece of wood keeps my bed up. There is a hole drilled through one corner and threaded with a loop of faded red four-millimetre cord. A long steel screw twisted through its centre, through and into my bed's cheap laminated end board and on into the central beam, holds rib-like slats in check. This piece of wood at the end of my bed is special, and without it my bed would collapse. Without this piece of wood, everything would fall apart. What makes this piece of wood special is that it fell from the sky and landed at my feet.

I would like you to imagine that my bed collapsed through frantic lovemaking, that I rolled and crashed with wild abandon on undermanned slats, my bed shortchanged by some Swedish accountant attempting to hit the right profit margin for budget beds. But it didn't. Most nights I sleep alone, my bed unmade, a bed no self-respecting woman would venture near to be fair: corners untucked, pillow slips missing, poppers undone. It is not what a bed should be. It's a bivvy most nights, unless my woman calls, then out comes the best silver – corners tucked (all four – hers and mine), pillow slips found, poppers done up. Most of the time my bed is just somewhere to sleep, not to belong, a doorway, a ledge, a patch of ground where the stones are small enough not to bite through your mat. It is a teenager's bed for a grown-up; one that is crawled into when you know you should have gone to bed an hour earlier, not run to with excitement long before it's time to sleep. In this bed there is no fun to be had, nor is it a place to linger. It is the place to kill dead the day.

It would be funny, in a BBC sitcom sort of a way, to lead you to believe that my raucous acts pushed the bed beyond its safe working load, only to admit later it was the jumping of my children that caused its demise. A bit of canned laughter to trick your mind into thinking that you're laughing as well. And yet my kids, although young, are old enough to recognise that cheap modern beds, made from ground-down trees, are not for jumping on. Old metal beds are best for this, beds that built an empire, that saved thousands in the Blitz as the roofs came down. The bed of a life should have a metal frame, metal springs, a net of metal intricately twisted into shape by massive metal machines long since dead or shipped off to China.

When I was a kid I loved sleeping under my bed. It was exciting. Beneath such a twisted steel tapestry there was a feeling of safety, from bombs that could bring down the walls, or reality that could tear down a life. Perhaps I'm not too old to do it again, although back then houses seemed much less full, and under the bed was not a place for wheeled storage boxes and 'stuff'. Back then under the bed was a magical place, a cut-price Narnia for poor kids, where you could shuffle in and fall asleep – and bang your head when you woke in the night. How many great minds found their calling looking up at the twist of the springs, questioning how each length of steel was bent and formed into the other like that, the ends sharp against their fingers and palms as they tried to grasp it all.

Under a bed you're safe. Under a bed you're hidden. Sometimes I'd like to crawl under my bed, but I never would – I know I'd only have to crawl back out, plus there's no room for me now.

So this piece of wood, where did it come from?

I was walking along the bottom of El Cap two years ago, close to the start of the *Muir Wall*, when I heard a dull knocking from above. The sound was not sharp and terrifying like a falling rock, a sound that my brain would react to with the same speed as I would the rattle of a rattle-snake at my toes, but rather something less threatening and more intriguing. And so looking up I saw something falling, bouncing down the wall, something that landed almost at my feet. A block of wood; four inches square, an inch thick, wrapped in a car inner tube, drilled and threaded in one corner with a loop of faded red four-millimetre cord.

It could only have come for a route like the *Salathé* or maybe *Excalibur*, a route with some monster cracks, designed to be stacked against a large cam, the rubber glued to the rock in the hope that it would help the wood stick to the granite – in the *hope*.

I looked up and couldn't see anybody, no telltale signs of a team, or the shouts of panic as the clumsy climber realised they were stuffed and would have to go it alone. The wall seemed empty.

I picked up the piece of wood and thought about just chucking it into the trees, yet another piece of big-wall flotsam, after all, who needed a piece of wood covered in rubber with a tie-off threaded through it?

I stood there wondering about its story – who had made it. I imagined them going down the lumber yard and buying the wood, or more likely pinching the wood from a skip. But then I couldn't ever remember seeing a skip in California, so I went back to the former image. The climber sawing the wood, finding the inner tube and glue, drilling the hole, bringing it here, laying it out with their rack in Camp 4, hauling it up the wall, leading the pitch with it clipped to their harness, unsure if it would work, dropping it and so making all that faff a waste of time.

And now it was in my hands – our paths crossed. It must have come to me for a reason, and so I decided to keep it.

So why did my bed fall apart? I'm not sure. Maybe it's due to me having rhythmic movement disorder (look it up), which means that since I was a baby I have rolled my head backwards and forwards when I'm asleep. It used to worry my mum no end. It would worry me if my kids did it too. But I guess it's a bit like being possessed by an evil spirit – sooner or later you either get used to it, or the spirit goes away. I don't do it that much these days, but it's so ingrained that when I do, I don't even know it, and I seem only to do it when I sleep by myself – or with my evil spirit. I can tell when I'm going to start doing it, as it tends to happen when I've completed my migration to the other side of the bed. When you've shared a bed for a long time you instinctively stay on 'your side', even when you're on your own. But when the other side remains empty, your instinct slowly fades, and millimetre by millimetre, night by night, you creep on to the other side. Maybe your body is always on the lookout for a bit of *Lebensraum*, perhaps it's the bed that moves beneath you, perhaps you're just looking for some love and only finding the other side of an empty bed. All I know is by the time I've traversed the bed, from right to left, my head starts rolling.

Anyway, back to the wood, and the bed. So somehow my bed was broken, too much shaking of a known sexual kind probably causing the two too-small screws that held the one too-large central bed beam to fail. It looked like a new bed was in order, but the next cheapest option beyond just sleeping on the mattress – and seeing as these days a bed is simply a warehouse for all the crap underneath it, why not just balance the mattress on all the crap underneath it? – was to attempt a repair; to screw a piece of wood to the end of the bed board and so hold up the central bed support. The only problem was, what to repair it with?

Like some Grecian tale of heavenly meddling in the DIY affairs of man, I realised that the piece of wood I'd found below El Cap must have been given to me for a higher purpose: to mend my bed. Digging through my box of climbing junk I fished it out and five minutes later I was once again the owner of a fully working bed.

Like I said, I don't really like my bed. Some days are for living. Some days are for remembering. Some days are for getting over with, and I see my bed as a switch: climb in and the day ends, and you go to sleep hoping the new one will leave you in better shape than the last.

But as I switch off the light, the last thing I see is that piece of wood – four inches square, an inch thick, wrapped in a car inner tube, drilled and threaded in one corner with a loop of faded red four-millimetre cord – and it reminds me of the wonder and randomness of life. That a tree could grow and be cut down, and a climber could cut himself a piece of timber from that tree on the other side of the world, not knowing that one day it would hold up my empty bed and have a story written about it.

4.21

UNTIL IT HURTS NO MORE

I once joked, standing by the kettle, that I could write a book about relationships. It was one of those things I'd say, threaded to a thought, that comes with the same planning, weight and suddenness as an unexpected sneeze. The girl I was speaking to burst out laughing at this, at hearing me say something so obviously stupid and un-self-aware, spraying me with tea in the kitchen. I stood there looking at this girl, feeling sad that she thought me such an idiot, that girl my girlfriend, partner, lover – whatever you want to call her, a woman not a girl really, but a girl to me. I guess that laugh was honest, and telling, because not long after we stood in the same place, my back to the worktop, my back always to something then, her beside the sink, no laughter, just a punch in my guts, her crying.

I think we all have stories like this, about that moment when love breaks down. I imagine some would rather not dwell on such things, bullshit mindfulness no answer, best keep such memories in the past, locked away in boxes or buried deep. I used to think I was good at this kind of thing, at compartmentalising as they call it. But it turns out I never was. You get the corpse of some bad feeling, emotional crap you can't deal with, dig it a grave and bury it as deep as it can go, bury it with distraction, hope it rots away and is forgotten.

I used to have a next-door neighbour who lost most of his skin in a fire, well as much skin as a man can lose and still survive. He looked like a Yorkshire Phantom of the Opera. If you go into WHSmith and flick through one of the books by Charles Bronson – the violent one, not the one from *The Great Escape* – you'll see a picture of that neighbour playing pool with Bronson, see what a state he was in. When you see someone like that, his face just about burnt off, you wonder how a person can take so much pain and survive. He's a model, a lesson, in pain. You wonder how you could live through that inferno, from that first lick, to the day when the pain turns to ash. But it does, flayed by flame one day, dead scar another, a man again of sorts.

One day you sit at the table and laugh with people like family, a clique of intimate knowing, and the next your name is a curse never to be spoken. Who wants to be a curse? Who wants to hold a curse in their heart?

Ella once said she didn't understand why with couples there is so much pussyfooting around ex-girlfriends and boyfriends, that she thought that once you're over you're over. But she's yet to fall in love, or have her heart broken, to box up her share of a life that once belonged to two. She is yet to understand the world, two senses missing still from its code: love and hurt.

We pussyfoot around, those of us who've had our hearts dashed already, because we know we're never free, we can't run from hurt, not really, not if we've really been in love or had something worth being bitter about. I guess it's like that old Joe Simpson question – is he lucky or unlucky? – to be hurt in love a sign that at least you once felt it.

Relationships are tough, hard to fathom, like a crappy script. Sometimes when we are so angry it's hard to grasp what is really there, what's driving those words, those emotions; me calling my ex-wife a 'fucking bitch' as I stamp up the stairs to get my stuff and leave her house, upset at some daft thing she said, that I'm 'not as articulate as Frankie Boyle'. We divorced ten years ago, and there we are arguing, me upset, her angry, her husband Mark staying out of it. When I come down and put my hand on the door I want to make my grand exit; I feel like I'm going to cry, but instead I reach down into the hole where that love and life we once had is buried in a shallow grave. 'I don't know why, but what you think about me means more than what anybody else thinks,' I tell her. 'She does say nice things about you,' says Mark, and I know she does, but never to me. But why should she? There is still a hurt that is yet to be forgiven, a hurt that has nothing to do with her.

Feelings don't heal like skin.

To make peace and to make amends takes time, a dangerous and painful act, to judge when that pain has passed. How long is that? Do you want to know? If I had to give an answer it would be the answer I was once given, an answer that sounded crazy at the time, of half that life you once shared. Only then could you hope to pass each other in the street and wonder what on earth you ever had. But for some the pain works its magic before they go. For others it's a wound that always weeps.

And if you rush it?

Sometimes you can push too soon for reconciliation, usually to ease the guilt, the forgiveness often nothing more than a clear conscience. You may have come to terms with the pain, but they haven't and so as you embrace, to make up, 'no hard feelings', you feel their blade in your guts, stabbing hard. And you have to take it, not back away, but let them open you up, until your guts are at your feet, and never stab them back. Let her, let him, let them, plunge in the knife until their hands cramp, their bloody fingers slip, the blade breaks; that they feel the pain they want to inflict is hurting them more. Take it like that well-deserved punch, because really it's only a kiss of a different kind. People do things that often seem strange, hurtful, murderous, beyond what you imagine people could do to one another when once they had so much love. But pain, inflicted or accepted, is often not so far from love as you'd imagine.

People love the idea that time heals, but really it only erodes I reckon, blunts the sharp edge of a painful memory, fills the hole vacated by joy. Time erodes until it's hard to grasp, this sharp bitter thing, then it's time to let slip. Grip it to you too tightly and one day that's all you'll ever have and ever be. To resign the most important connections in our lives – lips and tongues, sparkling eyes, held hands, laughter and ideas, supernovas of blissful emotion – to nothing but just bad memories, to wrap them up with all that hurt, disappointment, regret and rejection, and cast them down a dark hole of forgetting, that's not good. You should not bury something which many spend their lives digging to find.

So back to this book I wanted to write about relationships. What was I thinking! Yes, I've been a fuck-up, I've made a lot of mistakes, but then how else was I to learn, no real guidance from those around me when I was growing up. What does perfect look like? I grew up on an estate of single mums, fathers emasculated by unemployment, and violent and pissed husbands. A healthy relationship is like carving the Sunday roast in front of your perfect family, an operation learnt through trial and error, and a little blood. I've never carved a Sunday roast. No, that's all just an excuse. Relationships are simple really, all those hours of people ranting and crying in Relate probably distilled down on to a Post-it, even a stamp. My advice: find someone worth more to you than gold, who you know feels the same about you – you'll see it their eyes. Finding this person is not easy, but not as impossible as books and films make out. The hard part is not becoming complacent, letting that gold tarnish or corrode. That's often the skill we lack – I lacked. Gold is soft. It wears away. It needs to be looked after and polished.

The other day I had to travel back to the UK, an early flight better than a late one, a few hours to drive when I landed. But instead I flew late, first going down the climbing wall in Dublin close to the airport. Climbing up and down, taking turns with Vanessa, I kept looking at the clock, afraid I might miss another flight. Lowering off, with time for more, I just said, 'I think I need to go', to which Vanessa replied 'You've already gone'. Those words stuck in my head on the flight, then in the car, driving to the Lakes in the dark. Was that not always my problem? That I was never there before, but now I was; to be gone meaning at least I was there in the first place. To polish that gold would be to simply be there, so simple an idea, yet one so many of us fail to grasp.

But back to that kitchen at the start, that bad memory of a love breaking down. We talk now, me and that girl at the sink, the one who made me laugh so much, gave me more joy in so short a time together than she'll ever know. She has never been a curse in my house, my heart, or on the lips of anyone who has ever met her. Her name always a celebration. Maybe she knows this now, the words we sent not like at the start, no longer laden with hidden meaning or hurt, anchored in old pain that clings and pulls chains tight enough to snap. Sooner or later you have to respect the past, your choices, your complicity, be true to what seemed right. For a long time I suspect she thought she meant nothing at all, that she just filled a space between one love and another. She had little to spare you see, but it was so her to give me some anyway. But now the tears have dried, I hope she knows she is one of the most important people I've ever met; she showed me what it is to feel loved, to be worthy of someone like that.

And now? Now we both have others we can share our tea and jokes with, in other kitchens far away, people we may never have allowed to love us like we do if not for that short painful life together. Life's too short to let good people go just like that, to not acknowledge what they did, to be brave enough to say it, even if it's only in substandard *Grey's Anatomy* shit like this. That pain, life burning down, was just the transformation of both of us.

Some people are so bright and dazzling you can't help but reach out to touch, to maybe even hold for a time, but not always forever. If someone was worth the risk of being burnt, then they are worth forgiving of the pain that touch brought, the scars as well. When I said I could write about relationships back then, I think she misunderstood. In my mind I was thinking like a junkie writing about addiction, rather than as a nun. I knew little of what was right – how to have a perfect marriage – but quite a lot about what was wrong. Somehow she taught me enough to work out the good stuff, she set me straight. And so in that book I'll never write, there would be a short chapter like this, about forgiveness and healing, of allowing yourself to escape the hurt, like Charles Bronson, the film star not the prisoner.

I will always love her, that girl, that's why I think we need to come to terms. I will always be grateful, because she gave me something anyone who knew me then knew I was lacking: some small love for myself, that broke the link in that chain – to the past, to that relationship, the most important one of all, with myself.

4.22
THE BOAT

I'm haunted by the memory of a boat – half built and begun long ago, timbers now rotting, hidden behind a rain-soaked ruin and far away from shore. This thing, a skeleton of wood slowly growing soft, seemed to mean more to me than the sum of its parts. It spoke to me about the very nature of what pains me.

'Do you want to see my dad's boat?' she'd asked.

And so there it was, bigger than I could ever have imagined: not a boat, a ship. Too big to be laughed at; magnificently crazy and awe-inspiring in its ambition, a man's labour, his obsession and dreams standing there upon softening and weedy supports in long grass. No *Skylark*; a *Bounty*, a *Mayflower*, a *Mary Rose*, its timbers still oak thick and battered into shape by his hands alone; Frankenstein bolts, bloody with corrosion, holding whale ribs in their places, still naked without the skin of a hull. I walked its length, both moved and disturbed for what it represented.

'I started it in 1972,' he tells me later as we drink his home-made elderflower wine, feet up beside the open fire. 'It was just something to do – and I thought that maybe I'd sail away once I retired.' I ask about the size. 'Yes, I had no plans, and just started building it in my garden, but after twenty years it just got to be too big.'

He shows me pictures of the crane lifting this monster, and tells me of its long journey to the sea, becoming stuck for three days on some distant bridge, telegraph poles toppled. 'I still work on it,' he says, his feet up, watching the TV in front of the fire, 'but I'm too old to finish it.'

His boat sticks in my mind, the nature of obsession. I think about the tasks we set ourselves that are beyond us, the ones we will never finish, just frittering away life as if we were immortal, pouring ourselves into an unfillable hole.

'Dad, why don't you climb easier things?' Ella asks when I come back from the Eiger.

I have no other answer than, 'Easy things don't interest me'.

I'm reminded of sitting in a kitchen and talking to Alex Huber as he showed me pictures of his farm and his family. 'Andy, why do you make things so hard for yourself?' he asked. 'The winter, the novice partner, solo – you make everything impossible. It is as if you want to fail.'

But I don't seek out failure, or trauma or disaster – they're simply what you get when you try too hard, have too much ambition for your own good.

I don't want to fail. I don't want to fight.

'Half of what I own is yours,' she tells me after four years of working for her dream – our dream – when I tell her how I feel she has betrayed me, all the riches I felt would be ours, all hers. A dream it seems all in her name. I wonder what it would feel like to be as rich as her, to never have to worry about money again, but also to know that money is the only thing she can control – not time, not her body, not me. I wonder why I can't commit, to marry her, to feel secure. Marriage is all she wants; all the money in the world, but nothing without me. I think about sixteen years with Mandy, sixteen years she feels was wasted, working towards a future, building that boat in which in old age we'd sail into the sunset; a boat that was never finished. A failed marriage is a terrible thing; a house, all that stuff, all those boxes of photos, all those memories, all that time. To walk away with nothing, to start from scratch, no house, no savings, no future, to try and forget in order to have space enough to imagine something new. Once you've fallen out of love, had your heart broken, or broken the heart of someone you love, the scales fall from your eyes, and you know that all you believe will happen, want to happen, is that myth that keeps you going on – just the promise. I cannot commit to be married again, because I'm too scared that one day I'll feel the same – that this present certainty of the everlasting will one day wither away. I try and make her see how unfair things are that her river is in flood and mine is bone dry – that I put all I had into her dreams of glory – that I made her obsession mine. 'But I never asked you to,' is her damning reply. The first cut. Then she says she had never doubted we would be together forever, until now. Another.

I try and take it. We visit an ex-boyfriend. He lives in a huge house in the country: sports car, 'stuff' all around. He's a good man, but still just the flotsam and jetsam of someone's life. But as we drive away she says 'I think he's the one that got away' – another cut, perhaps the deepest, slicing into the most tender part of my soul.

Years later I told someone about what she'd said, and they told me that people say things without ever meaning what they say. But then and now I don't feel so inclined to give the benefit of the doubt, as what people say means more than they often realise. I think she betrayed herself; that deep down, she judged people not by what they gave, but what they kept. And I did not have enough.

The nomads of the steppe believed that possessions were for using, not hoarding, that life was a bridge that must be crossed, and by holding on to things, you made a house of them, which became a prison, and stopped you moving on. For the nomads, moving was life. I guess I've always felt the same, that if it came down to doing the sensible thing, or going on an adventure, there was no choice. So many times I've asked people to go away with me, and they've told me they've got some work to do and can't make it, trips that would stand proudly upon life. I wonder if they had gone, and I'd offered them the trade of what they had lost in money for what they had gained in the hills, if they would think it crazy to even consider it a fair barter. If the bills can be paid, the landlord happy, and you aren't starving, what else is there to worry about in an alpine-style life? What would you rather have: a month in Yosemite sleeping under the pines and creeping up the rock, or an Apple watch?

'If you asked me to marry you now I would,' she says, crying down the phone, but a week later I email to tell her it's over. It's the only way; I'm too much in love with her to leave, too wounded to stay.

As before, the years – eight of them – mean nothing, and I walk away with nothing. My stepmother asks why, leaving behind my home of four years, my imprint on her life so light my physical passing is simply the gentlest of leavings. 'That's who I am,' I tell her, knowing such things should never be asked for or taken, but only given.

Last night I talked to a bunch of salesmen in Stratford, feeling awkward and uncomfortable in smart trousers and shoes, and my shirt that makes me feel like I stick out instead of blend in. 'Are you a farmer?' two people asked, wondering if I was some kind of Jethro. 'No, I climb mountains,' I replied, as believable as telling them I'm a ballet dancer. A tough crowd, loud and with lots to say, they went silent as I talked, no yawns or whispers, no nipping to the bar. I told my story, from there to here, not your usual sportsman doing after-dinner speaking when all the games have been played, but a man who puts all he has into so little because that's all he thinks he's got.

Afterwards, the man next to me began to tell me how he'd never heard a story like it. He explained to me that I could do well, listing ideas of how I could be rich, a series of crazy stunts and plans. People joined in at the table:

'He could abseil off one of our thirty-metre cranes at shows.' I smiled and laughed at all their crazy ideas, blushed when they told me my story meant something, that I'm not like the others. 'You could die doing what you do.' In the end, I thanked them for their advice, told them that really I'm too busy juggling being a dad and trying to go climbing to ever make any real money. 'Getting rich is a full-time job,' I said. 'I'll leave that to Bear Grylls.'

The surf rolls in through a gap in the banks, sapped by winter storms and filling the lagoon with stones stolen from the Burren. 'Surfers are worse than climbers,' the man says, sitting in his kayak as we watch the surf sweep in soft and lazy at first, then barrel in hard against the shingle. 'When the surf's good they have to be there – they can't help it. Nothing else means anything to them other than the waves.'

Months after my email, unable to live without her, somehow, and beyond all reason or sanity, I almost find myself back, holding her hand in the kitchen, the beginning of a sad and tragic story one day I'll tell – write it all down where it may make sense. I didn't care about the past, what she said, what I thought she meant. Love was stronger than hurt. The cuts could heal with her love. 'My dad said I shouldn't get back with you, that maybe I'd lose half of what I have,' she tells me.

Another cut.

Fuck him. Fuck her. Fuck them all. All those that hate, all those that love, those that judge, those that understand, those that would see me damned, those that would see me saved. Those who say to move on. Forget. I hated her for not being brave enough to trust me, the man who had given everything to make dreams come true.

But she was right.

And out of anger, out of desperation, we find ourselves no longer loving each other, but fighting for what we both feel is right – for me to keep the home I lived in, and for her to keep what's hers, the balance equal after eight years.

I dig through hundreds of emails to prove to the court that I had an impact on her life, to prove I'm worthy of this grubby prize. It is emotional archaeology: digging down into the love, into the distance, the hurt, seeing the mistakes we made, the signposts, danger signs. What did I learn that I can pass on to you after so much digging? Love is strong, but it is not unbreakable; into the finest of cracks weeds can grow.

This is a lesson for those who find love's warmth, passed on by those who mistakenly thought its heat would be everlasting.

And then she calls me, and we speak for the first time in three months. 'Why are you doing this?' she asks. And suddenly I don't know why, dragging us both through the courts, where if I lose I lose everything. I'm not greedy or mean, and I know that a home means nothing to me, but perhaps I'm doing it to spite her dad, to spite myself, that if I am to be judged as being so bad a person, then that's who I'll become. But no. It's not that.

Unguarded, I answer. 'I can't let go – this is all I have left.'

I think a lot about that boat. I reflect on all the wasted time, all the money and effort, the sweat and graft, splinters and busted fingers – and for what? Can a life be like a boat, can relationships, built up with infinite love and care be then just left to rot? Do we hold on to what could have been, try and float knowing we will only sink, or just feel the sadness in its shore decay, see the folly of that ambition, of our love – or do we make a bonfire of it all, feel its heat, then start all over again?

4.23

EVEREST SUCKING ON THE BARREL

For some reason, I keep getting journalists – print, radio, TV – ringing me up and wanting my opinion on Everest, a mountain I've never climbed on a continent I've never visited. I'd like to believe this is due to my position as a world-class sounding board for the opinions of all climbers, but I put it down to a healthy Google ranking and a website with my email address on the front page.

Nevertheless:

Every time someone dies on Everest my mobile rings.

Every time there's another stunt my email pings.

Every time someone finds a pair of Mallory's old underpants I'm asked what this means for world mountaineering.

My stock answer is to point out I'm a climber, and that Everest isn't a climb, but a walk. This usually gets the person at the other end a bit confused and flustered as they check their notes. 'Yes,' I usually continue, 'if you have to step over a dead body halfway up then it's classed as a walk. On real climbs, the bodies fall to the bottom.'

'What do you think about the recent deaths?' they continue, ignoring what I've just said, their pen at the ready thinking one more quote and they can file their copy.

'Oh, dying is great, it's what it's all about,' I tell them. 'It makes it all so much better when you don't.' I explain the fact that every single summiteer will stress how 'undead' they are on their return – as well as in their book/blog/TV doc voiceover – weighing their achievement by the number of 'proper dead' there were. Sure, they'll speak to the BBC via satphone and say what a tragedy it is, but deep down they love it: it makes it real, gives it that edge, like sucking on the barrel of a loaded gun. If you summit in a year when no one dies, then you're forced to go back to 1996 and tell how eight people died in one day just to prove how 'undead' and hardcore you are. I'm told the figures for deaths on Everest are one in ten, which sounds bad until you consider the ratio between fuck-off scary mountain and clueless out-of-their-depth tourist. I expect if you dropped this bunch into Moss Side the numbers would come out the same – if for no other reason than walking around Manchester in a big yellow North Face down suit would lead to certain death by mugging.

Death and the risk of it is the stock in trade of many modern adventurers – just read my first book, *Psychovertical*, I'm nearly 'proper dead' in every chapter! – be it rowing the oceans (very safe, actually), skiing to the poles (also very safe), or running across deserts (ditto). Throughout all these things there is that Discovery Channel voice booming along about how hardcore it is, pointing out how X number of people have died while doing it. Well, lots of people have died driving along the M1, but they don't write books about it. Of course, no one wants to die – just give the impression they could. In fact, most Atlantic rowers have a support boat, and the last few high-profile polar trips had four-by-fours following them. But then mountains are callous and don't care about your backstory or dreams – or even how good you are. On Everest, the safety net that keeps you from the dead has very large holes, and the higher you get, the bigger they become.

These days when people get in touch my blunt answer to most questions about Everest is 'I don't give a fuck about Everest' – and no right-minded person should either. Who cares about the trash up there – have you ever been to India or Nepal, where a rubbish dump is called 'the other side of your garden wall'? Who's bothered about the fixed ropes, pegs and bolts apart from those who see them and have to trust them? You can't rape a mountain you idiot, only an idea, and when that idea is simply 'X is higher than Y', then who cares? What about exploiting the porters and the Sherpas? Again, have you ever been to a developing country and seen what lengths people will go to to make a living? Most of the hand-wringing by 'proper' climbers is all tied up with jealousy and the envy of opportunity, and everyone knows deep down they'd suck the devil's cock to climb Everest.

So, if you're a journo who's come across this bit of writing while doing your research, then please don't get in touch – although I'm happy for you to cut and paste whatever you like.

4.24

WORDS LIKE MORPHINE

Last week I switched off my Facebook accounts, hoping, but failing, to delete it from my life forever. Before I did, I wondered about downloading the archive of messages and comments, of which there were many hundreds if not thousands, giving me a digital bunch of letters from friends and enemies and lovers. But then why would I, what would that be? It's not like something my grandchildren might find in a drawer after I've gone, take off the ribbons and read, or a box of medals, or faded photographs, just a zip file. Fuck it, I thought. Just more junk I don't need. Move on and bin the joyless lot, throw it into the fire. But as I hovered over the kill switch, Facebook doing its best HAL impersonation, asking why I'm killing it, I hesitated. I went back one more time to my messages, scanned through them, looked at the questions, the 'best wishes', the 'minor threats' – nothing worth keeping. Then I saw his name, his avatar; his account still live although he was not. There were our parting words, that final message. They looked like all the others, but they were not. Those words had saved my life.

I know no one my age who has died of cancer. I must be lucky. I'm forty-five, and I guess my friends and those I know are a healthy bunch, and I'm sure this is not representative of most people. And yet I can count ten men who have killed themselves, probably double that if I want to dwell on numbers to justify what I write here, double that again if I include people who didn't want to live but whose deaths could be construed as in some way noble and heroic.

'*Did you hear…*' is occasionally how you find out, or an ambiguous news piece, how they died left blank, this strangest thing, this self-murder.

There is a link with cancer I think, in that suicide is viewed like we view the dreaded C; an aberration, a short straw, a bad hand when it is not, as familiar as life and as old as death. Like cancer it is something we are scared of, the spiders and snakes that lurk inside us, unsettling and upsetting, like anything that goes on behind closed skin, it becomes something 'other', only to be dealt with when we have no other choice and can't look away. Suicide's taboo comes from its early popularity, a quick way into heaven taken up with such fervour the church made it a sin. What is heaven? Is it not the bribe to stick around, to tough it out, to remain un-self-murdered? Consider then the power to combine the two, the murder and the heaven. Is the terror of the suicide bomber the bomb or the suicide?

The reason why the people I know killed themselves – by rope, by water, by bullet – look varied: a broken heart, a seemingly unfixable future, drugs, money. For some, it came as no shock, while with others it came like a bolt to everyone, a bolt so common you'd think such bolts would be rare. The reasons for going, and going with no warning, no histrionics, but just like that, may sound varied, but they are not. Their deaths were not the result of an inability to imagine things could get better, that this trauma would be short and fleeting, but rather the raw understanding they could not wait. To be that man on the edge is to be a man whose skin is flayed down to the muscle. You cannot bear the wide expanse of raw pain it would take for it to grow again. You jump from that skinless pain. Those left behind with the pieces, left by that most selfish curse, most often need a narrative simple and easy, skin to their pain: 'he was depressed', and that's it. Maybe only someone who's been flayed alive, flayed by others but often by their own choices, can know three words cannot do that murder justice.

The first time I got a message from this man on Facebook, his avatar popping up, this man's name well known to me, a hero of mine, a legend, I was shocked. No stories were ever his, no great images, yet he was often a key player, his name meaning more somehow due to his reticence to do more than simply participate. He was also a man out of the past, old now and broken down, breaking down further. His message was a simple one, braver than you'd imagine at first glance, about how what I was writing about at the time was helping him during a hard period in his life, helping him understand and come to terms with things. Only now, as I write this, do I wonder why he would tell me that?

What was I writing about back then? It was about the skinning of a human being, about hanging on as the new skin grew, bearing the unbearable. We struck up a Facebook friendship, and I was honoured to even chat to this legend, like Bob Dylan sending me a simple 'How are you today dude?', and feeling privileged he had read my words, and that somehow they'd had the leverage to lift some weight. Feeling this privilege, I took the time to try and understand who this man was, to look at his posts and pictures, to look in between his words, to see where this struggling man was going. What did I find? Well, if I had to write an algorithm to trigger intervention for the suicidal or those at risk I would input the age of the user with the number of Facebook posts and likes they make each day. Happy people do not hang out on Facebook. You know that, right? You need no calculations for that. Those are not shares, or likes, or comments, but a trail of lonely misery, a sob of tiny packets of data telling you – the world – that they are alone. To even sit in a car, on a settee, on a plane, and to visit that wicked place is to be self-isolated, to murder all that is living around you.

This man, my hero, was a man who felt at the end of things. You could tell; his words were staggering. He was looking back at summits knowing he'd never be up there again. His body was a mess; bones shattered over and over by the stones that had built his legend. I told him to write more, that he needed to move into himself, a place that I'd often retreated into, but he said he couldn't do it, this one hundred per cent physical man. He was a beast, a lion, his world one of sunrise and storm, of pine needle and sastrugi, the snap of karabiner and binding, not the click of a mouse or the rattle of keys. What do you say to such a man, a stranger a thousand miles away?

How do you save such a man?

'If only I'd known … ' people often say, but I think often we do know – think back to it. But we just can't make that leap from the idea to the doing, perhaps we too will be drawn in if we become involved. Just wait for the professionals, the therapist, the psychiatrist, the police, the undertaker. This is another curse to this wicked age that we outsource, we leave it up to third parties to fix, people who clock on and off. What happened to calling their mum and dad, brothers and sisters, friends? Give them meds, give them cells, give them lonely rooms with just two chairs, a cup of tea and a stranger to talk to. What about love? Worse still, we see it but don't have the time to step up; we have things to do, our busy lives making us somehow callous, the dead man won't die today. It can seem hopeless to intervene, most times impossible.

What can you do?

And then one day there it was, the story of his death, written in the beautifully respectful way that kind journalists and police officers from a small town can sometimes muster: a friend, a neighbour, a human being, not a stranger, of his great life and deeds, of his passing, but not how he passed. The lion walked out.

And there was that small curse, easily banished by nothing but 'he was a stranger, what could I do?' But it lingered that I had somehow failed him. I thought how like cancer we shy away, make ourselves a smaller target when it is close. Like Hail Marys, we say things like '*he had so much to live for*' – but we don't know. We cannot judge the kind of pain someone is feeling, so intense they give up their divine gift; no easy thing, no doubt the hardest they ever did.

What does it take to save a life? For me it was a stranger's email, asking if 'not to go' would be the brave thing, words that had more meaning, were more anchoring, more soothing than even the arms of my children. When you are flayed, you are not thinking straight, you only want it to stop, and worse still you feel those that love you will be spared your screaming. And yet it is the little things we do, the calm words, the hand on the shoulder, to steady, not the handcuffs, the pills and needles, the blunt probing into the past. When you hug someone tight and tell them not to go, you leave an imprint. It takes a lot to take a life, but it can take very little to save one.

As my finger hovered, ready to kill that Facebook virus and wipe our words away forever, I read that first message one more time, that message that came like a bolt from the dark. I had not saved him; he had saved me. My words, my screams to him, had been music, had let him know he was not alone, and in writing to tell me this – that I had value to a lion like him – his words were like morphine.

4.25

SHE WALKS AWAY

'She's got a nice body,' said Vanessa, nudging her head towards the waitress as she moved around the tables at the Banff Centre party, adding she'd seen her that morning in the swimming pool. I instinctively felt offended, my back straightening up righteously, lemon lips in angry pout, at such base objectification – sexist, misogynistic. But then Vanessa's a woman, so I was confused – cognitive dissonance they call it I'm told; that feeling, like being aroused by a woman on a bike while trying to pass her in your car, your base eyes on her great bottom, her long blonde hair trailing, only to see it's a man as you pass by.

Is it permissible for one woman to say another woman's got a nice body? I'm not sure, after all I've never heard a man say the same of another man, well, apart from a Bavarian lusting after my calves – apparently they have a thing about calves. I wondered if Vanessa had actually said to the woman, 'Wow, you've got a nice body', if she'd have been offended or simply seen it as a compliment? I know if I was told a man had said to his girlfriend that I had a great body I'd not have been offended, but then I'm wired up wrong. I wonder how a man would take such a comment in a swimming pool, like, 'Christ, you've got a nice arse', or, 'Don't you have nice skin'. I suspect you'd end up getting punched. Maybe Vanessa, being Irish, is somehow immune from causing offence, like a child. Irish people, long burdened under real hate and malice, seem to be able to recognise where the real danger lies in what we say.

I had a guy try and chat me up the other day while I was sitting trying to write a blog – which was annoying as I ended up having to talk to him, not rude enough to just reject a man's advances. He kept telling me he was from 'County Mayo' and I started to wonder if it was Irish code for 'fancy a shag?' I'm told I'm a homoerotic kind of guy, that if I was gay I'd be a bear – nice to know, if I was gay. I took this as a compliment but now wonder if it just means I'm fat and hairy? I told the guy that my wife was coming soon, and he finished his coffee and left.

It must be a burden to be beautiful, to have people hitting on you all time. Just this week I asked Catherine Destivelle, as we sat together drinking wine that came at thirteen dollars a glass, if it was hard being so beautiful, if it was a burden. She looked confused for a moment, then replied 'Me? Beautiful?', pointing at her bosom with her short finger. 'I don't think so,' she said, like a pro, something many beautiful people say, but only the truly beautiful believe.

I've always thought I was crap with women, but that was because I was crap at the beastly side of being a man, that brainless lusting and unsubtle dance that men tend to do. And then I got it – that you don't need to play that game, that it was effective just having a nice face, nice hair, a six-pack – that you never got a woman really worth the effort, not for all those sit-ups.

'You're really good at chatting up women,' said Al, maybe the most handsome man I've ever met.

'Me?' I said, pointing at my bosom.

'You just charm them.'

Vanessa says it's because I look like a pug, all soft and cuddly, while also a bit violent. She calls me her snuggle pug and warns me never to look into the eyes of any woman. To do so would have them under my spell.

'You're amazing at talking to women,' repeats Al, no doubt because he's so handsome he doesn't have to. I put him right, that the skill is what I'd call 'just talking', rather than 'talking to fuck'. In fact, the best way to chat up a beautiful woman is not to chat her up at all.

An example: the other night me and my mate Jon were sitting in a bar at 1 a.m. a bit worse for wear, just the two of us talking about books, neither of us the best cards, in fact both very bent and raggedy. All of a sudden this beautiful young woman plonked herself down between us.

'Are you a prostitute?' I asked.

'No!' she replied, a little shocked.

'Then why are you sitting next to us?' I asked. This was some form of rejection of her company, and so she stayed. She worked for Google and seeing as she was beautiful and we were not, we just talked. But soon enough more men appeared at the hunting spot, sitting around us, that 'can I join you?' really a 'can I fuck you?' to her, a 'can you two fuck off?' to us. Now the one thing young men respect more than anything is a great hunter, that's why women feel like meat. It's shitty and crap, but we're just animals. Get over it.

'The best way to chat someone up, well, a woman, is not to chat them up,' I said, adding the words 'a *beautiful* woman' – that being my first move.

'Go on,' she said.

'Well, the first thing you don't want is someone who knows she's beautiful, like she's doing you a favour, the reason being she'll be high maintenance, crap in bed, and make you pay for every second of your company.' Again this was a move. 'What you want is someone who's beautiful, both in body and mind, but mainly mind,' – another move – 'but who has a fabulous flaw that stops them from feeling perfect.' She leaned forward. 'You have a flaw, it's about your childhood, you feel like a faker, you've a beautiful mind trapped inside a beautiful head.'

'I've got a big cock,' interjected a bloke beside me.

Finding a woman, or man, is not – should not – be about fucking, it should be about seeking an ally, for one moment or many.

Have you ever played that game where you make a list of the three people you can have sex with without consequences? It's worth taking your time over the list, as although you're meant to have a free hand in the picking, I did meet someone who told me his included his wife's sister and his wife's mother – not a smart list. When asked myself, I realised I had two blokes on my list, which is funny because, as I've already mentioned, I don't find men attractive in that way. Now I know what you're thinking: who's on my list? Who are these two blokes? Calm down. My list is Tom Hardy, Michael Fassbender and a sandwich. I'm not sure why the last one's a sandwich, probably because it's funny, maybe it's a bit of a waste – although I have had some bloody nice sandwiches in my time. I think my list is just about spending time with someone, but maybe not Tom; I think I'd just like to fuck him.

Before I went on a date with Vanessa, I told her I had a sexually transmitted disease. I didn't, but how's that for a test of character?

Why we sustain, why she'll be my wife, is because she's unshockable, does not take offence – a good trait in anyone, another thing I love about the Irish. To be aroused by someone, or to be shocked by them, is a noble thing, be it in your loins or in your head, and yet I feel some – most – have become desensitised to its joy. Sex, loving or fucking is formed in the tussle of it, the same with ideas, to fight and to win or lose, that's what charms the pants. I've been lucky in my life to have known only women who did not quite know just what they were, would one day become; maybe their only fault their choice in men. This is a story about control, control over the mind of another, love or rape at either end, the stalker or the tale of love's persistence. We all believe that all we want is control, but we don't: we want to be out of control.

And so, the end of this story. I stand at the party, boys and girls out to find one another, music loud. A woman comes over and begins to talk to me, my pug face all charming. The waitress walks by, that waitress, and I say 'She's got a nice body', and instead of the conversation we could have had, written here, the woman lifts up her hand, shocked, and walks away.

4.26

THE ARTIST

Death comes by tweet. Death comes by forum, by Facebook post, by comment. Death comes by email or page refresh, breaking news or old-school text. Few learn of it these days by *'Did you hear ... ?'* or *'Did you know ... ?'*

But for some, death does not come unannounced, and that just makes it all the more tragic.

For some, an untimely death is almost an accepted certainty, part and parcel of almost every significant event in their lives, maybe even the very context of a life – the spice, the price. Their swashbuckling bravado in the face of it shocking, the living of which makes us want to turn away, but instead we press replay, our belief in their ability to escape the reality of an impending demise as delusional as theirs – even the greatest skill is no vaccine against the chaos of chance.

We watch and we all know it's coming, their long life not a thing to base plans on, their long life not a bet worth placing. We all know who these people are – people we watch, we love, who inspire, the best of us, but whose passing comes as no great surprise. A shrug down the wall, an 'only a matter of time'. We fake our shock, we tweet our sadness and share our stories of them, the stories never told, that fell between the cracks of their legend, little and big kindnesses that show they were mortal like us after all – while all the while, deep down, although there is the sadness, there is really no shock at all.

I will leave the poetry to others on this sad day, but it would be a disservice to the late and very great Dean Potter, and to the people who may wish to be swayed by those that eulogise his life, not to see Dean as the highly complex man he was.

I met Dean many times over the last sixteen years; at the bridge, on El Cap, in the cafeteria, talked to him, asked him questions, tried to get some understanding of who he was – because he fascinated me, just as he fascinated all of us. But Dean was ungraspable – the reason being perhaps because his greatest struggle was grasping the contradictions of himself: peace and anger, money and freedom, friendship and hate, playing the game while breaking all the rules, a shy showman, a man that wanted simplicity, and stability and certainty, but was tied up in the complex uncertainty of the hustle.

'What is Dean's legacy for the sport?' a journalist asks, and for a moment I feel angry, tell them that climbing isn't a sport, that if it was Formula One or bullfighting it would have been banned long ago, that there is no legacy worth the price, only tragedy, and that Dean's leaving robs us all.

When I first heard that Dean had started to describe himself as an artist, I laughed. It seemed like a very Dean thing to say. But when the journalist asks, 'What kind of climber was Dean?' – there it is. Dean was more than just a climber, a BASE jumper, a high-liner or a controversial dog owner: he was an artist; the mountains and walls his canvas, his spirit the brush. I am reminded of a line by Kurt Vonnegut that perhaps sums up Dean better than anything else: 'No art is possible without a dance with death.'

4.27

RABBIT STORIES

How real do you think you are? How much of you is a story, how much is true?

Have you ever heard the story about the rabbit and the scorpion? In this story a rabbit comes across a scorpion beside a wide river. The scorpion asks the rabbit if it can help it get to the other side. 'No,' says the rabbit, keeping its distance in fear of a sting, 'you'll just sting and kill me as soon as we get to the other side.' The scorpion replies, 'I promise you I won't, I just need you to help me'. The rabbit takes pity on the scorpion, drawing close so the scorpion can climb on to its back, and together they swim across.

This story popped into my head the other day while filming with Jen Randall. We came across a broken rabbit, dragging its long, half-dead body, legs trailing, numb to the earth, numb to us, numb to death, across the chalky rubble of the quarry floor. We failed to see it at first as we stood there talking, perhaps blinded by the fact it was not true to its animal nature, its paraplegia a slow camouflage, not jumping like it ought, nor speeding or darting away, but instead a furry caterpillar fast to the muck, its spine snapped.

We looked down at it while keeping our distance, some strange malevolence in its manner, watching as it moved inch by inch, alien-like, spiky claws dragging the muck, wondering how it got there. Perhaps by a fall from the cliffs above, perhaps hit by a car – the dual carriageway not far – perhaps by fright: a rabbit able to break its own back with the violent kick of defence. Jen looked down a little distressed, a more sensitive soul than I, an artist's heart beating, as the rabbit moved in slow circles, going nowhere, knowing it was done for I'm sure: dinner for a dog, or a toy to be shaken to bits. The story of the rabbit and the scorpion popped into my head, one I'd long forgotten. Then we went back to talking for a while, trying to ignore it there, knowing we'd not be able to do so, an itch in our thoughts, turning again and again to look at it, pulling its body by its front paws, on and on as if it believed some safe harbour may yet be found.

'Do you think we should put it out of its misery?' asked Jen.

Rabbits have always given me the creeps, not helped by the fact my cousin had the end of his finger bitten off by his pet rabbit Bobbles. My mistrust of these creatures was cemented in the early 1980s by the emotional tasering that was *Watership Down*, a movie experience I doubt any child from that era has ever forgotten. I remember sitting in a Welsh cinema with my brother Robin on a wet Saturday afternoon, watching a film that's like Francis Bacon does Disney, only with a bad dose of acid thrown into the mix – emotionally terrifying, an experience of tears and nightmare. *Watership Down* was not alone in its emotional impact, with *When the Wind Blows* and *The Snowman* being equally emotionally stark 1980s movie experiences. I've always wondered if what I saw in *Watership Down* was already embedded in my DNA, like the fear of spiders and snakes and heights and the dark, that rabbits hold some form of power over us of a substance we no longer remember, not the terror of the ratty rodent, but of something more pagan, and not only fear.

Ted Hughes was a man who cast spells through the rabbit and the hare, a man who also cast a long shadow over many a childhood; for me his book *The Iron Man* the crucible from which all stories of any value have risen: dark, harsh, austere, boundless and yet full of the music of imagination. *The Iron Man*, read to me at age six, was a window into an adult world of words far removed from children's stories. Hughes was a muscular thinker, his mind that of the beast more than the man, walking a dark path in search of verse and inspiration, a place few are brave enough to mine, no room for a liberal thinker apart from the day tripper, making him a fascination for the bohemian set, a savage of soil and blood, their very own Oliver Mellors. His lover Assia Wevill once said, having returned from an afternoon of sex with Hughes, that he smelt like a butcher, and it was perhaps the meat of this man that was and remains so enduring in our age of lentil thinking.

Hughes was an artist who saw the animal occult in nature, a black magic in all livings things, especially the beat of a woman's heart, and the dark pagan power given over to the fox, the crow, the hare. It's been said that this was a fad of his time, occultism and black magic just another hippy trend. But perhaps it was an echo of something timeless, a view of the natural world more in line with reality than one which sees nature as harmonious, that false-noble animal utopia, not the murderous and raw reality. There is an undeniable dark magic in Ted Hughes's words; they reach out, sometimes fur-soft, other times claw-sharp, the poet using language for both love and war.

Hughes, who was estranged from Sylvia Plath and his children, once wrote in a letter to his sister about accidentally killing a hare with his car and selling the body to a butcher in Holborn, buying red roses for his mistress Assia Wevill with the profits. Hughes adapted this story as part a play, *Difficulties of a Bridegroom*, about a man – Sullivan – rejecting his bride in favour of his mistress, and it was dramatised on BBC radio shortly before Sylvia Plath's suicide, the symbolism not lost on Plath, on such a poet's ear; Plath always the hare to Hughes's fox. It is strange to think in a world of such violence the power that words and stories still hold, of a simple story like that, written out and read aloud on the radio, drifting into Sylvia's fragile ear. Did Hughes know where those words would lead? Were they cast off like raindrops or poured slowly like poison? Did he know that beautiful and talented head of hers would lay down to die before her gas oven – perhaps in reply – as would Assia several years later, killing herself and her daughter. What Hughes wrote was as savage as any animal bite, and far more dangerous because the wounds of the sharpest words never actually heal over – such words are never forgotten. It's interesting to imagine how powerful a spell can be conjured up when the high art of poetry mixes with the basic act of an animal attack; interesting too to think that no other animal but man is skilled enough to kill with words alone – or unstable enough to take their own life, as Sylvia did.

I think a lot of the power of words, and of belief and stories. Most of the world is enslaved by these things, stories and words and trust and hope, the emancipation from faith perhaps the last great leap we need to make as a race before we can know true freedom. But maybe when that day comes we'll lose our soul, what makes us human, the madness that makes us beasts of our minds not beasts of the field.

But back to rabbits.

We watched it move on, never going anywhere, just round and around. Jen asked again if we should put it out of its misery, and I realised this was a question directed at me, not us.

A friend of mine, a physicist, was once healed by a 100-year-old Siberian shaman, his broken arthritic bones set anew by mushrooms and potatoes, rabbit fat rubbed into his naked body, and a rabbit's foot he carried until it disintegrated to nothing in his pocket. Not one to be taken in by such rubbish as this, he nevertheless decided not to question it either, a pain-free life worth a leap of faith by a man of science. I too have always mistrusted such New Age – or Old Age – ideas, spells that predate the oldest religions by millennia, but still on occasion you do get a feeling of what some would regard as magic. What are they based on, the woman on the mountain, the raven spirit, or the spirit of an idea you choose to accept? Is the power of words any different, is what that shaman whispers any different to what Ted Hughes wrote, words to heal or words to kill?

A Finnish woman once told me of a bone curse, a Sami curse, where you inscribe a curse on to the bones of a rabbit's foot, then wrap the bones tight with something belonging to your enemy and bury it deep. The curse increases in power day by day, month by month, slowly becoming part of the earth around it as it rots away, that horrible curse hidden from all but the one who took the time to think it and write it and bury it, the victim oblivious. When I asked how you wrote a curse, she said it didn't matter, that the curse was inside you, between you and the bones.

I thought a lot about the nature of this curse and curses in general after this, an old-fashioned idea but one I thought could be quite healthy if given a modern spin. It would be so much better for people to direct their pain and anger in such a way, to take all that rage and bury the pain, then sit back and wait for the outcome, which arrives sooner or later, bad luck and tragedy always just around any corner. So many people carry around so much bitterness and anger at others, I thought that by writing it down and wrapping it up with magic such dangerous thoughts could in some way be exorcised. But maybe the faith of the powerless is the source of so much religious voodoo – would a young man strap on a suicide vest if he had any real power over his life? Perhaps it is the reality behind all worship – of no value to those in need of nothing. The bone curse can only be lifted if the bones can be found, dug up, untied, scattered and broken – the curse set forever if the earth has swallowed up the curse entirely. Perhaps a warning that it is best to forgive before it's too late; to forget, a nice touch that has within it the importance of forgiveness over holding on.

The rabbit came full circle once more and we stopped talking and looked down, both no doubt wishing someone else would walk by and sort it out. Someone with compassion I'm sure would bundle it up and take it to the vet, but it was obviously past that, its bowels no longer working, some nasty end inevitable.

'Maybe we should put it out of its misery,' repeated Jen.

And so I found a stick, one of weight but not too rotten to break, not so light as to only whip, and walked back over to the rabbit. As I drew close, my heart set on the deed, our shadows met. All dead calm within the beast vanished, knowing in its small brain what was in my heart, what was to come next, the nobility of its animal suffering replaced by a sudden, wild, frantic scream of death, a whining, screeching sound that bled its horror into my heart, staying my hand for an instant. I hesitated, then brought down the stick on its skull with all my strength, killing it stone dead. I looked up at Jen. 'I think I want to cry,' she said. I tried to look cool about it, being a man and all, but like her all I could hear was the rabbit scream. I killed it as much to make it stop than to put it out of its misery – the real misery all ours.

Anyway, the rabbit and the scorpion. The rabbit made it to the other side of the river, the scorpion scurrying down off its back on to the bank, on to dry land. Then in a flash, before the rabbit had a chance to run away, the scorpion struck, its sting striking the body of the rabbit. As the rabbit lay there dying it looked at the scorpion and asked 'Why did you do that? You promised me … ' To which the scorpion replied, 'Because I'm a scorpion'.

How much of what we know is real, how much is a story? A damaged woman, soft and warm and real, killing herself. A myth wrapped in magic and words, a man of logic in pain wanting to believe in painless pagan magic. A curse sprung from a bitter heart, buried but not so easily forgotten.

4.28

AFTER HER

'I'm swimming across,' she says with a daring giggle, walking backwards into the lake, her emerald eyes reflecting back Tenaya blue, shoulders wood-brown from a month of Californian sun. I stand on the edge, pale, beside the narrow white rim of sand, the glacier-cold Tenaya Lake only up to my knees.

'It's freezing!' I shout sensibly – grown-up-like, killjoy – without a giggle, the distance too cold to bridge with a whisper. She pulls her comedy face, half frowning, half mocking pity. A goosebump wind slips down from Tenaya Peak.

'You'll freeze. Your arms will stop working.' I mumble-shout, unsure as the words skip over to her as she wades away, shout things I once read in a book about sea survival, some half-remembered line about how even the strongest swimmers can become immobile in super-cold water.

She throws back my concern with another mock frown: 'Do you think so?'

'You'll drown,' I shout. 'It's dead deep in the middle, it'll be even colder there,' I add, while knowing she is right to mock me. From the moment I met her, I knew she was way too hard – too bold – for her own good, the type of woman who's trouble – for all the right reasons.

'No I won't,' she replies, her words making me feel soft – justifiably so – and a worrier, that if she can swim in the Irish Sea in February, arms and legs beetroot purple, she's a match for any Tuolumne lake, no matter how cold. But then I look left and right at the tourists in the shallows, shivering, and see no one else venturing in more than waist deep from the thin shoreline, thinking that they probably never did.

She waits, head turned back for me, waiting for me to come. I move a little closer. She begins to come back, closing the gap. I hesitate, get the fear she's going to splash me, then wonder if she plans to wrap her arms around me and pull me in, pull me out, into the deep, drown me for a laugh.

'I'm scared,' I whimper, stopping and wrapping my arms around my shoulders, acting the child, feeling the water still only up to my thighs, but so cold all I want is hot sand and the warmth of a towel. The phrase 'balls deep' pops into my head as my scrotum darts inside, giving it new meaning.

'Well I'm swimming across,' she says, turning to face the other side of the lake, a good 600 metres across its dark heart. I stand and watch, unable to stop her as she wades further in without hesitation, the muscles along her sides in rhythm with every step, moving like an animal, feet dancing on the bottom, her body weighty and dense with the movement. She has that way about her, as if anything is possible, that her limbs could wrestle with any sea or lake monster she might find out there.

The climber Richie Patterson once said that when I walked, I looked like a man who couldn't be killed, that I seemed unbreakable. It was something that sounded cool and stuck in my head, like a prayer – a little rabbit's foot for when times were tough: *I'm unbreakable, I'm unbreakable – Richie told me so.*' I never understood what people meant when they said I was 'like a tenement block' or 'built like a brick shithouse', I just thought they meant I was fat. I didn't understand until this year, until watching Johnny Dawes walking around, a bit out of shape, but still streetfighter sharp, gypsy tough, not a man who could be pushed, that maybe that's what I looked like.

Now when I watch her move, I see it too. I wonder if this appearance comes from a kind of animal confidence that some people have, that there is no questioning the body's physical capacity to deliver, no physical doubt whatsoever.

With only the lightest flourish – and no hint of hesitation – she dives, her dark brown hair swallowed by endless blue, and she is off … fearless.

Again, I stand and worry, worry that she may not make it. I look back at the kids on the beach. I wonder if the water is so cold due to the melted snow. I wonder who I'll call if she never comes back. I wonder about all the hassle – and about telling her mum. 'Selfish bitch,' I mumble to myself, half joking, half cross, totally in awe of her toughness.

When we'd first got together I'd gone down to the sea with her, her 'towel carrier', but it was the Mediterranean that time. I'd only known her a short while and was still pretending to be a real man – after all, that's what all women really want, even if they say they're happy enough with boys. I said I'd go in, even though I hate swimming, hate the water – especially cold water, something I put down to being washed into the sea on Boxing Day in 1975, caught by a wave in a game of chicken on a boat ramp on a stormy day. I lost the game but was saved by my dad.

On that trip to the Med the water was still winter cold. I'd stripped down to my shorts but had only gone thigh deep before I found myself fixed to the spot, realising no woman – even her – was worth another inch. I could live with the shame. I watched her plough on in as well-dressed French dog walkers in fur coats looked on in concerned surprise. I walked back up on to the rocks – trying to look manly – and put my clothes back on and waited, and waited, and waited some more. I couldn't see her anywhere, not behind the rocks nor out in the sea, just an empty ocean. Fuck! I thought she must have drowned ... what a shame, I quite liked her. It didn't seem worth making a fuss, or going for any heroics – jumping in, etc. – after all, I'd read it was the last resort in that book about sea survival. But then she appeared, out of the sun-dappled water, corpse cold. I soon found out she quite liked it.

And so now I stand again, watching her head move slowly away, thinking how strange it is to be the worried one for a change – the one left behind – worried that someone you love will set off somewhere and not come back to you. Is this how it feels? I wonder, her head now pinhead small, arms ploughing through the water, while I stand alone on the shore.

I need to interject here with an admission: this is not a story about me, but about her. Ed Douglas – a man who has dissected me better than anyone – once told me, 'You are a constant source of fascination to yourself. It worked for Proust, so own it, don't deny it.' Ever since then his words have stuck. Every time I write, I know it's true, that in a lifetime of obsessions – climbing, writing, films, people – I was my greatest obsession of all. Why shouldn't this be a piece about other people? It is for you, the reader, but I'm sure you'll get bored. Maybe that's why I go away and do crazy stuff – seek out the 'tough' – not because it gives me things to talk about, but because it helps to further illuminate myself, stops me getting bored with me. But then, to paraphrase Werner Herzog, 'who likes a fully lit room with no dark corners?'

And here's another admission that comes to me as I write – which is maybe why I write as much as I do, why I'm the subject: all my life, which has been by and large happier than most and free of any real tragedy so far, I have always been shadowed by a sense of impending calamity which colours everything. If I were to put my pig-farmer-psychiatrist's hat on, I'd say it's born of poverty early in life, from events beyond my control, where even as a child I was aware how exposed I was. Perhaps that's why I climb such scary things, how I can deal with it, because I've found ways to manage the low hum of fear all these years. On a big wall or alpine face, there is always the danger, but it's a danger you can cope with – come to terms with – and so even in the most terrible of places, that sense of impending doom retreats. You go from the notion of 'this is great, but what comes next?' to 'who cares about what comes next? This is great.' Yes, you can deal with the steep, but not with the flat – a very common malady. But with her, from the moment I sat down beside her in a Dublin pub and asked if she'd ever had a broken heart, I knew she had something, something I'd only found when close to death on walls and glaciers and faces. Something I needed and wanted, something she gave; something I was scared I'd lose if she didn't come back.

And so, to my surprise, I push on into the deep: hip deep – chest deep – shoulder deep – then just deep. The water is stunning – and I'm stunned I'm actually going after her. I swim for a second then stop, unable to breathe, and just wait, wait to either begin breathing again or not. My breath comes back, just a bit, and I swim on – breaststroke, the only stroke I know.

I move slowly, the water now black, and try to focus on something other than the cold; I make up a heroic story to focus on instead. I imagine I'm swimming at the North Pole, in an open lead, setting a new world record, Discovery Channel cameramen and crew in a safety boat close by. They'd no doubt ask why I was using breaststroke over the more traditional hard-man front crawl, to which I'd reply, with Bear Grylls's intensity, 'keeps the hair dry, vital for subzero swimming'. But I realise this is just making me feel colder.

Her head has now disappeared completely, the far shore no closer, the distance to shore behind me unknown, me too scared to stop and look. I try to think about hot things, everything I can think about: fire, lava, the sun, apple pie heated in a microwave for eight minutes. I think about the Grand Slam bomb, the largest non-atomic bomb of the Second World War, the 'earthquake bomb'. Made in Sheffield, they heated up the high explosives in kettles before packing them in; it took a month to cool.

The wind picks up, small waves splashing me in the face, water into my mouth. I feel a slight panic, but lift my head and spit it out, looking for her as I do. She is nowhere to be seen. The shore is still no closer.

I think about the Hoover Dam, how when they built it they had to feed in water pipes filled with ice-cold water to cool the three million cubic metres of concrete it is constructed from; that if left uncooled the concrete would still be warm 125 years later. I imagine myself now, not out here in this cold dark water, but down in the depths of the dam, like some entombed immortal waiting a million years to be freed by the erosion of time. Entombed, but nice and warm.

I think about the brazen bull used by the ancient Greeks and the Romans, a hollow bull into which a victim would be placed and a fire lit underneath, a kind of metal trumpet inside designed to transform their screams into the sound of a bull. I imagine I am Perillos, the sculptor who made the first bull for the tyrant Phalaris, how he boasted at the sound a man would make when being roasted alive, which so disgusted Phalaris, he asked Perillos to climb inside and demonstrate, only to lock him in and light a fire; Perillos, the first victim of his wicked machine. I try to imagine the cold I feel is not cold at all, but the rising heat. I try to imagine what it would have been like inside that bull – terrible, but also distracting.

It isn't working.

I can feel I'm slowly losing control of my hands, my feet are dead, all heat withdrawing into my core. Again I feel a twinge of panic, that now I must be halfway, too far to swim back, too far to shout for help. I am scared about getting too tired or getting cramp. I haven't swum more than half the length of a swimming pool for years; I'm depending on survival fitness – the fear of drowning giving me the edge to make it across – 'sink or swim' as they say.

I think about my mate Espen Fadnes, how he'd undertaken months of cold-water tank testing when at university, how he'd learnt that if he stayed still in the tank and let the cold creep down his arms and legs until all that was left was the embers of life in his core, he could stay in longer than anyone else. A few years later he landed in the winter waters of the sea in Norway when a BASE jump from a hotel went awry. Unable to climb out he knew he'd succumb to the almost subzero water if he tried to find an exit, and so he just floated there until some passers-by spotted him and dropped him a ladder. When he climbed out he was so cold he could only hook the ladder's rungs with his bent arms.

I look up again.

There she is, pulling herself out of the water, on to the slab about 200 metres away. She looks tired. Fuck – if she's tired!

I pick up the pace.

She sits with her knees up shivering, a huge surprised smile on her face as I splash the last few metres until my hands drag over the hot sandy granite.

'Polar Bear, are you OK?' she asks, as I paw at the rock, arms utterly dead, legs unable to push me up.

'I don't think I've got it in me to get out of the water,' I gasp, reaching out a pathetic hand.

She doesn't move.

'Sure you can.' All she offers.

And of course, I can ... and I do.

We lie on the slab, hoping the weak sun will warm us up, bring us back to life. She is shivering while I am just frozen. I would cuddle her, for my benefit more than hers, but I know she is corpse cold – how she likes it – so I don't. She could take it. I lift my head and look back over the water, the sun about to dip behind the mountains. Soon it will be colder still, without even the sun to warm my head.

On the far shore I can see Ella and Ewen lighting a fire for our return – illegal of course, in the national park – but a nice thought nonetheless.

'Fuck. How am I going to get back?' I ask out loud, looking left and right, wondering if I could bushwhack back sans shoes.

'I'm swimming back,' she says. 'Well, after I've warmed up a bit more. You can do what you want ... '

I lie back down and move closer to her until our dead-cold skin touches. I think how much she means to me already, how much I need her. Then I feel the edges of it, that sense of impending doom, the doom of love; that it will leave you, or you will destroy it if it stays too long. It's not real, this feeling, just a symptom of how my mind seems to work. I wonder how she can be strong enough to take me on, then think how this had all started with me at my worst, at death's door, and every day she has closed that door a little more. Most relationships start as an act, where we put on our best show, the act of being who the other wants us to be, then slowly – toothpaste on the sink, socks with sandals, tempers lost and tears – we show our real side. We let down our guard. I realise that from the start I only had the energy to be me, the last man standing, the man you'd not want on your team.

But she has picked me.

I wrap my little finger around hers.

She slips down into the black water, looking as dubious in her return as I had at the start, giving a shiver as it swallows up her brown shoulders. Smoke rises from the far shore, no doubt soon it will attract the Feds.

I look down into her green eyes, startling – her smile, honest – just happy. I watch her hand rise up and reach out, not to pull me in, but to take me with her.

'You coming?' she asks.

'Will you wait for me?' I reply.

'Sure, Polar Bear,' she says, that mock concerned frown appearing for just a moment, before fading away as she sees I am genuinely afraid. 'Of course I will.'

Like I said before, I hate the water and hate the cold. I'm a wimp really.

I am forever in fear of some calamity befalling me. But with her, I don't feel it. With her, with Vanessa, I just feel everything will work out.

And so I slip back into the water, and we swim back to the far shore together.

Bad Poetry: POLY WALL

10,000 miles

and half a life

I still reach and feel

that Fabergé hold

on a wall

no longer there

& pull.

5
UNIDENTIFIABLE

5.29

ROGER GODFRIN

I hate to be distracted when I'm writing and have an idea for a story, this one about a boy who didn't do as he was told. And today, writing this, I was interrupted.

It began as it most usually does, with that question: 'What are you writing?' I told the old man it was a story about the war, a story I thought I knew, but on reading more I found there was more to know, more that could not be known.

He had been in a war.

I closed my computer.

We talked about death.

'On the way to a funeral you must throw a penny at each crossroads,' he said, hunched and ancient as if a heavy life lay upon his green duffle-jacketed back.

'Why?' I asked.

'That way the dead can find their way to the other world of course.'

'The Romans buried people who'd committed suicide at crossroads,' I added, wondering if there was some connection between the Romans, the Roma and this old Irish traveller. 'But they called it "self death" not suicide back then.'

'Once upon a time they'd bury you at a crossroads with a wooden stake in your heart, like a vampire, if you committed suicide. It was a sin,' he said, his chunky thumb smoothing the side of his coffee cup. 'Be interesting to know how many kill themselves these days compared to back then, now we don't have sin any more.'

The old man finished his coffee and left me to think about death and sin and missing his company.

I cut what I've already written and paste it below our meeting. I begin again.

The village of Oradour-sur-Glane was once a beautiful and peaceful village set in the lush farming region of what was then Limousin, France, beside the river Glane, which sang 'under deep green cradles its eternal hymn of glory to our beautiful Limousin'. Farmers and their families would come into town to buy supplies, to visit the market, perhaps stay at the hotel or visit the cafés. At weekends people would play football and fish, or go to church on a Sunday.

In 1944 Oradour-sur-Glane was a small island of peace set amongst the chaos of war, the day Saturday 10 June. The allies had landed in Normandy only four days before. The world was in flames, tens of millions dead – but not in Oradour-sur-Glane.

The town was busy that Saturday morning, its inhabitants swollen from 330 to almost 700; refugees from war-torn regions, hidden Jews, red Spaniards who'd fled Franco's Spain. People had come in from the countryside, some to get a promised tobacco ration, others for their children's First Communion. A medical visit had also been scheduled for the children, so 191 boys and girls sat waiting in the school.

The whole world was at war, but at that moment life in Oradour-sur-Glane was a picture of peace.

Then at 2.45 p.m. ten trucks loaded with German soldiers drove into the town, 180 men from the 3rd Company of the Waffen-SS Regiment *Der Führer*. They disembarked, their weapons drawn, and advanced into the town. Most of them were younger than eighteen years old.

Their reason for being there varies depending on official and unofficial accounts. The day before an ambulance had been found with the occupants burnt alive by the maquisards, the French resistance. A bridge had been blown up. An officer had been kidnapped. Oradour-sur-Glane had been chosen by mistake, the neighbouring town of Oradour-sur-Vayres – fifteen kilometres away and full of resistance fighters – the real target. What is known is that the SS were attempting to get to Normandy, the balance of the war at play. If they could defeat the Allies at Normandy, which they had a very good chance of doing, the landings being a huge gamble, then it would mean a total defeat of the British and the repulsion of the American threat for many years to come. It was a fight to the death. But the maquisards had risen at Charles de Gaulle's command to slow the German army, to give the Allies time to create a bridgehead. The maquisards had done an impressive job of stalling the enemy, the journey from Bordeaux to Normandy not taking three days as it should, but seventeen. For Charles de Gaulle this was not so much simply a fight for a free France, but his opportunity to define himself as the saviour of France, having already undermined the 25,000 communist partisans in Paris. The truth of why the SS were there, or how things unfolded, will not be known until 2053 when the sealed account of what happened will be opened, but what is known is they were there for murder.

The town crier was commanded to bring the whole village to the square so that everyone could show their papers. Men and women and children, the sick and the old, no one was exempt. Soldiers went from house to house, pulling out those who had hidden, the school teacher appearing in his pyjamas, the baker naked to the waist and covered in flour. Soldiers searched the houses for treasure to steal, for maquisard weapons and explosives, or their lost officer Karl Gerlach.

The women and children were split from the men and taken to the church, while the men were split up and taken to six locations.

What happened next is unclear, as most of the German soldiers involved would soon be killed in the war, and most of the town's inhabitants would not survive the day.

At around 4 p.m. there was a huge explosion, or a series of explosions, in the church, at which point the soldiers guarding the men opened fire. The church was now in flames, the screams of the women and children heard as the soldiers went amongst the men shooting the injured in the head before setting fire to the bodies. Six men somehow survived beneath the corpses, and wriggled out and escaped into the countryside, all were burnt and shot, but alive, and sure their wives and children, mothers and fathers and brothers and sisters, were dead.

Of those in the church, only one escaped, through a window. Some say that the Germans placed a bomb inside the church to kill them all and then shot those who tried to escape, while there is also evidence that ammunition had been stored in the church, and this had somehow exploded, creating the trigger for the massacre. Regardless, the murder was done. Oradour-sur-Glane was set on fire and destroyed, and by the day's end the village was no longer part of the eternal hymn of glory to beautiful Limousin. To this day it remains a ruin, a monument to war and its 642 dead.

I go to Wikipedia to check dates and times and places and numbers, to double-check the dates in my head. I take a moment to chide the internet for being so hysterical about Trump, thinking – at that word 'hysterical' – how I'd read that morning about a woman left unmurdered by a serial killer, the reason being that she knew hysteria at being bound and raped would see her dead.

My laptop battery at seven per cent, I visit another site before finishing up.

I see that 'Oradour' comes from the Latin *oratorium*, which means an altar. The town is at a crossroads and in Roman times had been a burial ground. Oratorium: 'a place to offer prayers for the dead.'

But my point, I almost forget.

When the Germans arrived they went to the school, and the children all lined up at their teacher's command, lined up and filed into the square to 'assure their safety', then up to the church and to a horrific death. All died but one – Roger Godfrin – a young boy who disobeyed, who listened not to his betters, those wiser than him, but to his animal spirit and instinct, who on seeing the Germans coming said to a friend, 'They're Germans, I know what they're like. They'll try to hurt us. I'm going to try and escape.'

And he did.

5.30

HOW DOES A CLOCK TICK?

I received a direct message this morning:

> *Steven Seagal films are funny? Steven Seagal is a great actor and a great martial artist you little prick! Go fuck yourself! If I ever saw your moron ass on the streets, i would kick your ass! His movies are great you dumb little prick cunt faggot pile of low life shit!*

It made me think of B-29 bombers.

If asked what was the biggest industrial military project of the Second World War most informed people would say the Manhattan Project, the weaponisation of the atom, but they'd be wrong. In fact, the most expensive project was the development of the B-29 Superfortress high-altitude bomber. The US military realised they needed a heavy bomber early in the war, one that could bomb from high altitudes beyond the range of anti-aircraft weapons and fighters, plus one with a much greater range. And so the B-29 was rapidly developed, to attack both Germany and Japan. Although no expense was spared, the bomber arrived too late for the European theatre, but soon enough to devastate Japan with both conventional bombs, incendiaries and two atomic bombs – which incidentally killed far fewer than incendiaries. As an aside, it was here, in the war with Japan, that we first really understood the jet stream, where these high-altitude bombers found they got nowhere, even under the full power of their Pratt & Whitney engines, once up in the opposing jet stream.

The B-29, along with the atomic bomb, won the war against Japan, the first destroying the cities as well as the ability to fight – but not to die fighting; the second removing the noble delusion of mass suicide and honourable slaughter. I wonder if anyone who fought against the Japanese, or who was defeated by them, found Obama's apology for dropping 'the bomb' a misreading of the logic of its use, the death of some better than the death of many or all.

During the war against Japan, Stalin's Russia remained neutral, his war against Germany war enough, Japan well known as a formidable and dangerous foe by the Russians. And so Stalin offered no harbour to American bombers, forcing the Americans to carry out raids from India and China, some of the longest and most dangerous raids of the war. The Americans also developed the B-39 bomber, designed to attack Germany from the US if the UK was to fall, and the Germans did the same with their Amerika Bomber project, actually flying a bomber from Belgium to New York to check the feasibility of dropping a German atomic bomb.

Stalin knew of the B-29 programme and asked to be given these aircraft several times under US military aid programmes, but each time he was refused, the B-29 the state of the art in terms of military and aviation technology.

Spies in the Manhattan Project had given Stalin plans for the atomic bomb, but the B-29's complexity was beyond stealing, and almost beyond even Boeing at the time, which was still grappling with such an advanced aircraft. Stalin could see beyond the war with Germany, that the war would continue after the fall of Germany, that his allies would quickly become his enemies, the war simply a break in the greater struggle, that the very reason for the rise of Nazi Germany being America, France and Britain's hope that Hitler would check Stalin. (General Patton and many others pushed for the Allies to defeat an exhausted Russia as soon as Germany was defeated, knowing they would never again have so many men under arms in Europe.)

Stalin knew that only through military strength could he keep the Western powers at bay after the fighting ended, and so a heavy state-of-the-art bomber was crucial for his defence, giving him time to rebuild and renew a primitive and devastated industrial base.

Luckily for Stalin, B-29 pilots were told that in an emergency they could attempt to reach Vladivostok and land there, and three B-29s did just that during the final months of the Pacific War. In each emergency landing, the pilots were interned and the aircraft impounded, with neither being returned when requested by the Americans; the pilots were eventually allowed to 'escape' to Iran.

With these three aircraft the Russians began the most complex and audacious reverse-engineering project ever – unless we did snag a UFO in Roswell – dismantling and copying an entire aircraft, perhaps the most complex machine of its time, containing not just cutting-edge manufacturing technology, but also the most advanced targeting and gunnery computers yet made.

Russia's strength then – and still now – lay in a very tough, utilitarian and practical approach to design problems, a creativity born from necessity: the T-34 tank was a war-winning design that in no way approached the sophistication of the German panzers, but it did not break down and it could be manufactured in the tens of thousands. To be handed one of these aircraft and told to copy it was like handing an iPhone to a blacksmith and ordering him to produce a fully functioning exact copy and competitor – by next year, and on pain of death.

And so with no choice, one aircraft was slowly dismantled, one was used as a reference to the mountain of parts, while the third was used to test the aircraft in flight.

The problems involved were immense, the most basic being that the Russians were working in metric while the US worked in imperial; a small problem you'd think, but not when every single available item from nuts and bolts, to wiring and sheet metal and slide scales, were all out. Every part was weighed, measured, mapped out, drawn, blueprints made, then tools and new methods created to make them. Even simple things like a Plexiglas window was far beyond anything ever seen in Russia. Another issue was the use of aluminium, something not readily available in Russia, leading to a need to create a whole new industry in alloys – although Russia did have most of the world's titanium at the time. Many parts of the aircraft were beyond anything seen before by Soviet engineers, including computer bomb sighting and guns – which were remote controlled – and every tiny fuse, transistor and circuit required a monumental degree of engineering.

Throughout the project, which involved hundreds of thousands of people and all areas of industry, failure was regarded as treason, a firing squad or a trip to the Gulag for anyone who could not see their part through. Of course, the Americans knew that the Russians would attempt to steal as much technology as they could, but a whole aircraft? Such a thing was impossible, and yet, just as the CIA believed the piecing together of documents shredded as the US embassy fell in Tehran in 1979 was impossible, again they underestimated their foe's will, as well as their adversary's brutal approach to the solving of an impossible task.

Then, on the afternoon of 3 August 1947, as American diplomats stood watching the annual Aviation Day parade at Tushino Airport, they heard a familiar drone. Looking up as primitive Russian fighters passed over, out of the gloom came a flight of what appeared to be the three captured 'B-29' bombers ... and then a fourth appeared. It was the Tu-4 bombers, the 'Bull', a copy of the B-29 so perfect that in the end it weighed a mere 350 kilograms more than the original.

If you want to know how to act, how to direct, screenwrite, edit, do stunts, create convincing sets and costumes, in fact, any part of the process of making a film, you can watch Scorsese, Coppola, Herzog or Hitchcock. Or you can watch Steven Seagal. Here, laid bare, is a masterclass of the imperfect, the murder of what a film could be. Digging down into a career, you start with *Under Siege* and slowly work down Seagal's opus. We begin with films of fair quality, then quickly enter his blue period, straight to video, then to DVD, then download, then Netflix, YouTube, then only Russian and Middle Eastern TV stations, and finally the bin. These films are a gift to the aspiring filmmaker, the very absence of anything, in any department, that could be viewed as being even sub-standard – in fact there is no standard – is a lesson that would be much harder to learn from a master. And yet they were made that way.

And so by a time machine spurred on by this blog, I got a message. Let's read it one more time:

Steven Seagal films are funny? Steven Seagal is a great actor and a great martial artist you little prick! Go fuck yourself! If I ever saw your moron ass on the streets, i would kick your ass! His movies are great you dumb little prick cunt faggot pile of low life shit!

It would have been fun to reply to the message, but the sender blocked me. If I'd been able to reply I'd have thanked him wholeheartedly for his words, after all it's a great piece of writing, and I'm not being ironic. It has weight and magic and spirit, is worth framing, and more important, it's ripe for deconstruction. And so what do I see in its nuts and bolts? I see the true talent of Steven Seagal.

Yes, he dresses like Kim Jong-il, has spray-on hair and an ego that could not be digested by even the largest black hole, but he invokes violent loyalty. Would anyone but our mums write such a thing in our defence? Probably not. No, Seagal is the Zen master; he's got more 'slosh' than most, his world more balanced than most. Yes, we can smirk and snigger at such clowns with their macho posturing. Know without a shadow of a doubt that him and his ilk and followers are fools – drinkers of Starbucks coffee. That we are better than him, more perfect. But it's us that are deluded; he's laughing at us, wasting our lives in search of perfection, tinkering and adjusting each component of our reality in a quest for that perfect balanced copy, while Seagal flies in a fifty-tonne travesty to taste. He flies still.

One day, we may wake to find our smug world, so near perfect, has such an imperfect and tasteless man in charge. Imagine that.

Everything can be deconstructed, bit by bit: unscrewed and unhinged, weighed and measured, to see how it works, how it ticks. But first, you need to *want* to know, to ask the small questions in the hope of the big answers. This is me writing out such a process of engineering, an aggressive message, taken apart, word by word. It's what I like to do. But I'm not that good, as look here; fifty-two words have turned into one thousand eight hundred and forty-one.

But again, how does it tick?

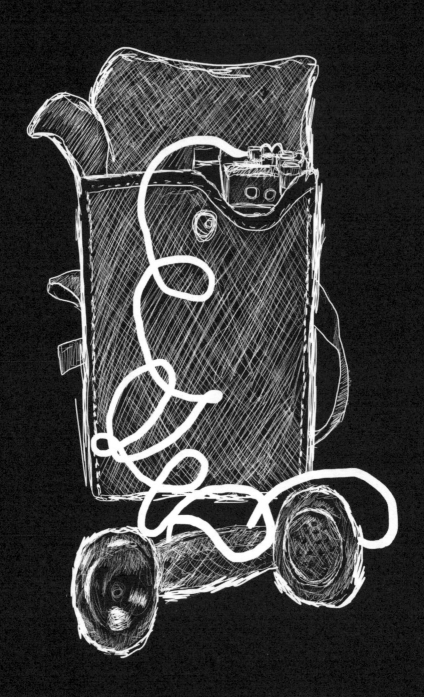

5.31
LEARNED HELPLESSNESS

The CIA are masters of interrogation, their techniques exported far and wide, used by their friends and their new enemies. Torture can take many forms: water, sleep, a commercial meat slicer, the rape of your child in front of you. It comes in many flavours, the most brutal of which is nothing to do with the information required, just base terror. CIA interrogation manuals discuss the issue of helplessness, characterised as 'apathy', the result of prolonged torture: 'If the debility-dependency-dread state is unduly prolonged, however, the arrestee may sink into a defensive apathy from which it is hard to arouse him.' The technical term for this is 'learned helplessness', the result of inescapable 'aversive stimuli', the outcome being that the subject gives up the fight and simply becomes the victim.

Genghis Khan was one of the first rulers to really grasp the power of psychology over an enemy, that they could be defeated by a weakness of the mind rather than a weakness of arms – a necessity when Khan's adversaries outnumbered his own forces. Khan's weapon of choice was simple terror. He created a myth that moved before him, of a juggernaut of crazed fighters, an unstoppable 'horde', no army or city able to resist, whose dictum was, 'surrender or die'. In reality, Khan was highly exposed and could often have been defeated, especially from the rear, having no army to hold what he had already captured, his empire at its height twice as large as Rome's. Early in his campaigns Khan would make an example of a city that resisted; upon gaining entry, he would kill almost everyone, then make the most of this investment in time by pushing the few survivors forward before his army. This way the news of Khan and his bloodthirsty horde, drinking blood – they did, but only of their horses – was carried from city to city as refugees tried to escape. He further tricked and defeated his enemies by having his men drag ropes behind their horses in order to create huge clouds of dirt, giving the impression of a much larger army, and his men always lit three torches at night, not one. The ability of boys on horseback to defeat vastly larger and more sophisticated armies by using simple terror of the mind was equally well employed by ISIS in Iraq when a ragtag army of 600 jihadi fantasists in Toyota trucks defeated a modern army of 6,000 in Ramadi in 2015. Some say Khan killed tens of millions of people during his reign, over ten per cent of the world's population, and maybe he did, but maybe such a figure simply demonstrates the power of terror, that 800 years later it still does him great service.

The use of propaganda in modern warfare – the word propaganda first used extensively by the Catholic Church in the sixteenth century: 'Congregation for Propagation of the Faith' – came at the beginning of the First World War with the 'Rape of Belgium'. Most of the population saw the war as nothing to do with them or their countries, a Serbian archduke murdered of no concern, especially to Americans. But after the German invasion of Belgium, again of little concern to the British or Americans who were used to small European wars, it was Charles Masterman and his War Propaganda Bureau's 'Report of the Committee on Alleged German Outrages' that galvanised world opinion. It switched focus from a power play of kings and queens to a 'highly stylised' telling of murder, rape and torture of innocent women and children, much later viewed as containing 'perverse sexual acts, lurid mutilations, and graphic accounts of child abuse of often dubious veracity'.[1] The report spawned sensational articles and books, with the writer William Le Queux describing the German army as 'one vast gang of Jack-the-Rippers'. The eagerness to fight Germany by the mass of the population, rather than just the political class, can be primarily laid on this single pamphlet. By war's end, over eighteen million people were dead.

The use and sophistication of propaganda and psychological warfare, which we now call public relations, has increased exponentially since 1918; Adolf Hitler and Joseph Goebbels its next masters. Hitler was aware the German army had been partly defeated by propaganda, and was aware he would need its power to coerce the German people to his cause. Through the power of words, of radio and film and print, he could sell the people a myth, a fairy tale, with simple slogans and ideas, room to live. We're all children really, all love fairy tales, complicit to the theft of our free will, and who could resist when the greatest talents of the age were set against us? Again, the desire to fight had to be sold, as well as the desire to fight back in wars far from your home or your own self-interest. By this war's end, sixty million people were dead.

---

1 Nicoletta F. Gullace, *The Blood of Our Sons* (New York, 2002).

The Vietnam War was a turning point in the business of control, popular media taking the fight out of the population, the realities of war, its base nature beamed direct – a 'live' war. The youth had willing minds ready to be mined, still half children, that firm belief in a man coming down the chimney once a year still fresh enough and ready to be replaced with other illusions. The old know certainty is unaffordable, that truth is a compromise of competing realities, but not the young. They are always searching for revolution and new meaning, happy to opt for the simple explanation that 'The Man' is behind it all. And so the Americans were not defeated by their enemies in Vietnam, but by the effectiveness of the propaganda of their enemies at home, no press around to televise what came after. The old were overthrown by the young. But one day those agitators for change would grow old, take power themselves, and be forced to find new ways to defeat such childish ambitions.

In wars to come, the Gulf wars in particular, but also Czechoslovakia, Chechnya, Palestine, control was reasserted, lessons learnt. Media was either coerced (it had to 'get with the programme'), intimidated (most media of the twentieth century was either a shop window or a game of sausage selling so that was easy), sidelined or crushed (a bullet in the head, the slandering by media already corrupted). News became entertainment, emotional porn, bought and sold, combined and amalgamated. Now there are two narratives, Left and Right, two realities that few seem able to traverse. Journalists are just workers, they have families and mortgages, they want to move up, they play the game – after all, who wants to report the truth when their only source is a blogger with 100 followers who lives at home with his mum. As Adam Curtis stresses in all his films, a simple narrative was created in the 1980s for incredibly complex relationships, the reason being they were an easy sell to people without the time to think. Ask yourself, how much difficult material you can sit and watch these days, Curtis's *Hyper Normalisation* documentary beyond most people's attention spans. We just have too much to do to think – but what is it we think we're doing?

A prime example of how the system worked is Gary Webb's 'Dark Alliance' pieces in San Francisco's *The Mercury News* in the 1990s. In this he exposed how the CIA were funding Contra rebels in Nicaragua by selling Columbian crack cocaine to black communities in Los Angeles, leading to the 'crack explosion'. At the same time, the CIA were engaged in selling weapons to Iranians – against their own arms embargo – in return for the release of American hostages, the funds from these sales going to the Contras. Gary Webb's efforts to expose a monumental and criminal abuse by the state met with little support from the major newspapers, his reporting criticised and undermined. Webb was destroyed as a journalist, and in 2004 he was found dead, suicide – with two bullet wounds to his head. This led some to believe he'd been murdered by the CIA, but such simplistic readings let off 'the system' and how it works – again, a simple narrative. Webb wrote: 'If we had met five years ago, you wouldn't have found a more staunch defender of the newspaper industry than me … And then I wrote some stories that made me realise how sadly misplaced my bliss had been. The reason I'd enjoyed such smooth sailing for so long hadn't been, as I'd assumed, because I was careful and diligent and good at my job … The truth was that, in all those years, I hadn't written anything important enough to suppress.' In 1998 the CIA inspector general revealed that for more than a decade the agency had covered up a business relationship it had with Nicaraguan drug dealers in LA.

And now to these future wars, Syria and Ukraine, the war for global power, Brexit and Trump vs Clinton, wars whose propagandists have difficulty in figuring out how to use propaganda against you, but have an almost limitless supply of money and talent to try. The gas attacks in Syria by Assad, complete with dead children, are straight out of the Rape of Belgium notebook, a 'line crossed', but who takes the time when that one fizzles out to go back and discover the rebels gassed their own? I sound like a conspiracy theorist here, but have no doubt that the fourth estate – TV and print media – is utterly corrupted, both by the nature of being only shopkeepers, but also because we have been fed propaganda for so long we are like robots. A BBC journalist living in London or Manchester has to be locked into one way of thinking, otherwise they just cannot fit in to the 'correct way' of thinking. Have you ever wondered how in free media we have to choose between Left and Right channels, why we can't get both from one source? It's because people take sides to fit in. There is rarely any consideration that their position could be wrong.

To have thoughts and ideas from someone else's code is almost impossible. We are blind to our conformist way of thinking, a clever trick someone must have played on us, the moment we find anything that does not fit in this landscape we've created – my old dogma of certainty – a button is pushed. Our response, if analysed logically, betrays how well we are manipulated. You start any debate with someone, try to break their grip on this reality they've been sold, and almost immediately their warning lights go off, their sensitivity so heightened to any threat to what they've bought into. The other night I disagreed with someone's piece of writing, a feminist reading of the normal interactions of men and women in climbing. In the space of one paragraph the other person jumped from accusing me of 'mansplaining', to women being murdered and raped – a subtle charge idea that to even reject what she was saying could make me either a rapist or a murderer or complicit to that end. One thing in this war, is that we are being divided very effectively, men against women, old against young, rich against poor, the faithful from the faithless, black against white. Broken down again and again by some hand. The politics of identity are utterly self-defeating to the greater aims of man. In fact, how do you feel about that use of 'man', does it offend? And why is that?

And now we have the fifth estate, the web, a place that is much harder to sideline, a place once 'out of control'. The system is trying to exert control now, first by using the classic three techniques of white, grey and black propaganda: white – omissions and emphasis; grey – omissions, emphasis and racial/ethnic/religious bias; and black – commissions of falsification. It is also applying pressure on organisations like Facebook, Twitter and Google to rig the code; banning users and so denying them a platform – on a charge of hate crime most usually, or choosing what is shown and what is not shown. The web has been flushed with false information – 'fake news', false fact, so many sites defending their side while attacking the other – which you cannot trust either. Try doing a search for 'Google manipulates searches'. First of all, what are you searching on? Google, right – yep that's an issue there! Try doing a search on Google and then on Bing and you'll get different results. Up there you'll find the snopes.com site. Click the first link – 'Google Manipulates Searches for Hillary Clinton' – and scroll down and you'll see a big red X to show it's not true. But then many fact-checking sites that are popping up are not impartial. Now I don't believe this particular story is true but it does demonstrate the technique of disinformation: nothing can be believed.

And now we are bombarded – day by day, hour by hour, minute by minute, second by second – with stories of hate, violence, racism, sexism, homophobia, that 'Not all Trump supporters are racist, but all racists voted for Trump', that with a single election all laws were abolished. Fifty-one per cent of Brits are bigots – including the black and Asian ones, people wearing pins of support for the newly oppressed. People are ashamed to be white in a country that is eighty-two per cent white, but then if you're a woman then it's OK, you're simply suffering from 'internalised misogyny'. Jean-Luc Picard says this is the worst thing to happen in a hundred years, and rational people agree with him. Sir David Attenborough quips of Trump, 'We could shoot him'. The news is full of stories of rape, of football players texting bloke crap, and idiots calling Michelle Obama an ape make it to the front page. People tweet stuff like, 'My one year old asked if we're all going to die mummy?', a slow but steady drip, drip, drip into society's ear. Hate. Pain. Anger. Sadness. Tears. Share. Retweet. Repeat. Repeat. Repeat. And so people begin to switch off. They log out. They stop taking notice of what is going on around them. It's just too painful. But what is the 'system'? We are.

And how do you feel now?

Empowered or helpless?

5.32

DOG

Stimulus.

The ball is thrown.

A dog that barks is afraid.

Does the name Pavlov ring a bell?

'How do you train a dog?' I ask as we walk, this farm girl no doubt a pro.

'I have a shock collar,' she says, just like that. She explains how it works, small shocks only, to correct the dog's beastly nature, to run and bark, to attack and shag.

'Did you know that apart from dogs we've bred out the disobedience from our animals? Over 10,000 years we've killed the troublemakers, the aberrant, those that resisted the herd, that didn't come at the dog's bark or shepherd's whistle. Now we have only pets and meat.'

She looks at me as if that was an unfunny joke. Her phone buzzes.

I was once bitten by a dog owned by a man called Bull. To feel an animal's teeth press into your flesh is a strange thing, primordial; you don't forget it, even at five. Such an event is a main line to the raw code, to the beginning, the big bang inside us all. That's why we love sex, not for the coming, but the going back to the bang – the raw and real bang.

'Can you imagine what it would be like to kill someone?' I say at the breakfast table, like a teenager would talk about forming a band. Everyone looks down at their eggs and sausages. 'I was once bitten by a dog,' I say, embarrassed. 'Like a werewolf bite I've never been the same since.'

See things through the eyes of a dog that broke free:

Buzzzzz.

'Jeremy Corbyn cheered by racists and terrorists.'

Buzzzzz.

'Dutch woman with two British children told to leave UK after 24 years.'

Buzzzzz.

'One million migrants heading this way.'

Buzzzzz.

'Why psychiatrists are speaking out about Donald Trump's mental health.'

We see a dead child on a beach and we whine.

We see Gaddafi with a bayonet stuffed up his arse, a bullet in his belly, naked on a road strewn with Hellfire dead, and we pant.

Eighty-six people are killed by a truck and we bark 'Iraq' and 'Bush' – good dogs.

The Trans-Pacific Partnership is killed and even those who'd die for the cause of anti-globalisation just sit.

Buzz. Buzz. Buzz.

I deactivate my Facebook pages. 'You're being stupid,' I'm told, 'look at all your likes.' I consider what I gain from those pages, how they're partly how I make a living, that without them I'm afraid I might go hungry. I hold my finger over the button and think of the cost to me, and then of the *cost* to *me*, and just like that, a couple of thousand likes go down the drain, like marbles I once imagined valuable, only lumps of cheap glass.

Buzz. Buzz. Buzz.

Someone starts messaging my publisher on Twitter to inform them that one of their most successful authors is a misogynist. What would be the hoped-for outcome for such a thing, from a man who'd be steaming open letters or sticking black tape over images of women in another place? We are being policed by ourselves, what once required re-education and Gulags, now nothing more tame than 'like' or 'retweet'. The Gestapo are our 'friends'.

Buzz. Buzz. Buzz.

Friends send me links to bring me back to the party. They worry about my mental health, find my views upsetting. How can everyone they know think and say and act the same but me?

Buzz. Buzz. Buzz.

'You'll lose all you've worked for.'

Buzz. Buzz. Buzz.

I get emails, people telling me that I'm 'brave', braver than them, to keep it up. I get money, donations, the visitors to my words only increase. How can that be, this climber with notions? Am I what some accuse me of being, are my allies those I hate?

Buzz. Buzz. Buzz.

I consider that I really am going mad. How else can I explain the reason I see things the way I do? Am I chasing my tail? Will I need to put myself down before I bite?

Buzz. Buzz. Buzz.

Then my mate Rob ends a 'how are you doing?' email with one beautiful treat:

Al was at my place, first thing he said in the morning after the US election: 'Andy K predicted this ages ago … '

The collar loosens.

I am not a mad dog, and so I warn anyone that will listen that we really need to begin to question who our real masters are, who holds the lead, gives the treats, kicks and starves and kills. Does that sound crazy?

Bbbbbbbbbbbbbbbbbbbuuuuuuuuuuuuuuuzzzzzzzzzzzzzzzzzzzzzzzzzzzz.

But let's finish as we started …

In the Second World War the Russians trained dogs to blow up tanks. They starved the dogs then put food under their tanks, which were static at first, then with their engines running. Mines were designed to fit on to the body of the dog, with a wooden trigger stick that extended upwards like an aerial. The second it struck the weak bottom of the tank it would explode, killing the dog and destroying the tank. A noble sacrifice for the motherland by a Moscow stray. And so they marched to the front, against Nazi tanks not Russian, and set their super weapons loose. The noise of combat was terrifying, and some dogs ran back and jumped into foxholes killing everyone, while others who tried were shot by their own side. Some dogs pressed on, their desire to eat overriding everything else. But these tanks before them were different, looked different, sounded different – their machine guns blasting, smelled different. The dogs sniffed the air for Soviet diesel, smelling instead only German gasoline, until they caught the familiar scent on the air, behind them, their own forces, and so ran back swiftly to feed.

Not long after being bitten by that dog that belonged to a man called Bull, a pit bull jumped into my baby sister's pram. Imagine that, what fear that lays down. 'The dog died,' my mum told me later. It jumped up on to a lamppost and hanged itself by 'its own collar, caught on nail'. I had a vision of that, in my five-year-old mind, for the rest of my childhood, like the page of a loved fairy story, where you know every single detail. Then one day I realised, just like that, that mad dogs that jump into prams don't kill themselves.

I look up electric dog collars to see how they work, or if they're even real, hard to imagine in this soft age. There are the words: Shock, Fear, Correction.

That dog man Pavlov again:

During chronic experiments, when the animal, having recovered from its operation, is under lengthy observation, the dog is irreplaceable; moreover, it is extremely touching. It is almost a participant in the experiments conducted upon it, greatly facilitating the success of the research by its understanding and compliance.

Do not be afraid of the dog that barks, but the dog that does not.
Who throws the ball?
Response.

EPILOGUE
WHAT I'VE LEARNED

Not Your Man

If you want a filtered, branded climber, I'm not your man, unable to supply that Instagram snapshot that prevails these days, all pressed and clean and made over; sending cool projects, yoga in the meadow, mock-Buddhist karmic bullshit and snappy quotes set over pictures of waterfalls or small puppies. If you want that, I'm not your man.

Wanking

Climbing is like masturbation: it's fun doing it, but no one wants to hear about it, and that's how I approach the subject. It's a personal experience, and I find there's little of any interest writing or talking about it, so if you read on don't expect too much of the C word. For me climbing is about something richer than crimps and pull-ups.

Sex

Everything in life is about sex apart from sex, and the same applies to climbing, which for me is complicated; far gone for me are those halcyon days of first love.

In the Clouds

I was high for much of my childhood, 'my head in the clouds' as my mum would say, living in a block of flats in a run-down northern city after my parents divorced. Hull had made its fortune from great shoals of cold cod and the slaying of whales, all in deep decline in 1970s Britain. My mountains and wilderness were the bombed-out buildings from the war and the wreckage of recession, rusty cranes and bridges, and the docks in which we swam. It was here, in this urban wilderness, that I learnt the art of the daredevil, skills I later took to Antarctica, Alaska, Patagonia and Greenland, poverty and necessity giving me an edge others often lacked.

Suicide

They say it's darkness that sets apart the super elite from the elite, that you need something bad in the mix to have that little extra. I don't think much of anything was ever done by a happy, balanced person, after all why bother when you have bliss? Well, apart from yoga poses on Malibu beach.

The previous tenant of our flat hanged himself on the stairs, a death that haunted my childhood, too much for a sensitive young soul. So right from the start I guess there was that foundation of rope, death, gravity and suicide.

Beholding

'You're too poor to have principles,' someone once told my mum, to which she replied, 'no one's that poor.' It stuck, and has perhaps held me back in life, that I never ever wanted to sell out to my principles; happy to be me, not Bear Grylls. For most of my climbing life I've run away from any form of proper sponsorship or shabby money-making, preferring to work for my supper, not beholden to many – plus the more you earn the less you climb.

Hard

Climbing harder is easy. There is an industry built around telling you how hard it is, but it's not. All you need to do is climb three times a week, stretch, remove the fear of falling, eat and sleep well and achieve a healthy weight, and find a good partner to support you on and off the rock. If YouTube or Rock and Ice leaves you unsatisfied with what you have, buy one of those 'How To Climb Dead Hard' books, or a yoga mat.

Wild Animal

Climbing is a wild animal. It can be fun and playful, but forget that fact, turn your back on it, and it can chew your head off.

Back

Never turn your back on yourself. Be honest, be who you are, not what you think people want you to be.

Expectations

People generally have low expectations when it comes to speaking, so don't disappoint.

Burnt

Love is a fire. It can start with just a spark, it can rage, it can warm, it can heat you so hot and wholly you feel you'll never ever be cold again. Yet never forget that one day it could be a bonfire of teeth and limbs and laughter, a forest of hope with which to feed the fire, and then – only ashes. Love can burn your whole world to the ground.

Love

Never take it for granted that those you love the most still know you do. Take the time to tell them so because one day you may find them gone. We're brave people aren't we? We hang from cliffs and walls, crap into a paper bag without even a blush, so why do we sometimes lack the strength to simply say how we feel, to text the words, 'If I had to choose between breathing and you I could hold my breath forever'?

Leaving

Never mistake anger for fear. When you are chased out of the house when you choose to go away, it's not anger at your leaving, it's the fear that you may never come home.

Reality

A does not follow B. There's a space there, between the letters, between the words as you say them. In that space there is time to consider the past, the present and the future, why you began there: at A and not X or G, and why B needs to come next. I was never good at remembering the alphabet and maybe this is why, and I'm not good at following the same old familiar path down which most ideas lead, the places school, our parents, the media would take us. My thoughts and my ideas, my politics, what I believe, are ambiguous, to me and others, and that's how we should all be as nothing is static, not the now, not the past, not the future.

Lead

When instinct leads you to an answer you need to ask yourself why. If you follow your instinct – what you've been bred to believe – you often take shortcuts to answers that, although comforting, are wrong, and so all you think and believe is built up from these simple false truths. We surround ourselves with like-minded people so as not to question what we believe, and marginalise or demonise those that don't think like us. The unsimple truth is that reality is too complex and ungraspable for most people – after all, who's got time to consider all the data? If you consider yourself a liberal, and have a liberal world view, then you're going to be half wrong about most things, and the same goes for anyone right wing. Our human brains, fed so much information, so angry and enraged, ready to 'like' and comment, and believe our opinions matter, really are nothing more than a series of shortcuts designed to reinforce the unreality of what we think we know. It takes practice to break away from these shortcuts; you need to get into the heads of people you hate, to think their thoughts, see their reality in all its complexity, the scared cop with a gun, the addict breaking into your house, the racist burning down a church, the pirate, your mum, your dad. The problem with this kind of 'breakout' is that very soon you find you're a nomad in your own head, no safe harbour or real belief beyond that you really believe nothing. Instead, like Superman, you hear all the world talking at once. To go to such a place is as scary as any Patagonian spire, but just as necessary if you wish to really grasp what you are – even if the answer is nothing at all. We are ultimately irrelevant. Not something easy to take and that's why we have God, phone-ins, 'like' buttons and comment fields.

Dying

You never hear the one that gets you, but when you are about to die – or think you are – do you know what it feels like? No anger, only the deepest sense of disappointment, like waking from the greatest dream you ever had, only to realise it was just that – only in death, well, near death, it's that in reverse.

Life

Live life on your terms, and seek out what makes you happy. Be selfish, because if you're selfless and miserable you're no good to anyone, just another unneeded martyr. The single proviso is that your pursuit of selfish happiness must not rob anyone else of their happiness – which I guess is what could be seen as the fundamental balance of life.

Fucking Up

You're much more the result of your fuck-ups than your triumphs, as most triumphs lead nowhere, just dusty trophies. Mistakes on the other hand always lead somewhere good in the end. Yes, you may feel crushed in the cogs of life sometimes, but at least the cogs are moving.

Madness

I find myself out of rope thinking I've reached the end, talking to a crowd of people about climbing again, my life in ashes – because of love and climbing I tell myself, but really because of me. Afterwards, and almost too distracted to notice, I sit beside a young woman in a pub, her sitting beside me because I am the 'guest climbing speaker'. Making small talk she tells me about how much she loves climbing, boring details of crimps and jams and talk of routes I have no way of knowing. But with her the words seem to mean something: honest, light, full of hope and goodness. As she speaks it feels as if the vice that is slowly crushing me eases off a little, and I find myself there: completely, uncomplicated, listening instead of thinking. 'Do you have a broken heart?' I ask her, and she says 'yes.'

V

And so it goes. I sit at a picnic table in Camp 4 with her, who, like climbing, has taught me a better way to live, that there is no need to see everything so dark and twisted, that for us there could be that unfiltered Instagram reality together – only without the yoga. I know I'm not an easy man to love, that I'm high risk, unable to resist the beat of the darkest drums, self-regarding and always in want of more, but hey, I'm an artist, dude! But I'm brave, and tell her there, at the table, chalk dust on our hands, that for all the good and the bad that climbing has brought, what you the reader can see between the A and the B of my words, all the pain and sacrifice and joy, 'if there has been some great unseen purpose to it all, it has been to lead me here to you'.

NOTES

1.1 The Land of Green Ginger

One of the biggest mistakes a writer can make is to think they're any good. Writing is like learning to ski – the moment you think you've got it, you crash and burn. To carry that analogy a little further, in writing like in skiing you need both speed and caution, to throw yourself over the edge and let go, while being aware of how easy you break when you fall. My dad once told me that the more you wanted to stay dry while kayaking (switch sport now) the greater the chance you'd get wet – basically not caring about going in helps you be better at not going in. Anyway, this has nothing to do with this bit of writing, but the second biggest mistake is to have an editor who only thinks you can reach a low level. Ed Douglas once said my biggest problem is that I'm cleverer than people think I am, which is perhaps down to how I look (like a bin man), or the way I act (a fool), when really I'm a bit of both, plus a bit of something else (someone or something far too serious). And so when I was asked to write something for *The Walrus* magazine in Canada I was blown away, *The Walrus* being a big deal over there – and not a climbing magazine. And so I penned a story that at the time I thought was great stuff, being half about this teenage trip to a bunker and half about Greenland, visiting another relic of war. The idea had been one about light and dark, past and future, but when I reread it I only liked the dark part, maybe because it's different – and different is good. What this taught me though was that as a writer you should set your own standards, and not give up until you've done your best work – not just the work someone else thinks you're capable of.

1.2 High Marks

This was maybe the third piece of creative writing I ever did, about an early repeat of a route called *Prore* (Scottish VIII). I seem to remember I wrote it one evening, then had it published in *Climber* magazine in the UK, *Climbing* in the US and maybe *Klettern* in Germany. The structure of it would be used later on in *Psychovertical*, as would the words themselves in the form of a prologue. This bit of writing is very much the template for the kind of writing I like; it has lots of space and not a lot of detail, and the reader fills it all in. It's also about climbing and not about climbing. What sticks in my mind about this is that about a year later I did a talk for a climbing club, and afterwards someone came up and introduced themselves. He said he was an English lecturer and how he thought this piece was perfect, and how he used it in his class. At the time I was a little embarrassed and laughed it off – but it had a big effect on me. You see although it's good never to believe you are a good writer, that what you write has a place in a universe full of words, you nevertheless have to believe that one day – if you keep at it – you will be. For someone to validate that I had something of value was just the talisman I needed to keep on going.

1.3 Broken

If I ever had a breakthrough piece of writing it was this one, and in some way this was my university, a writing programme that took two years to complete and resulted in this. The reason it ended up quite good was that I lost it several times (I didn't know about undo changes!) and had to keep starting from scratch, so all the dross got left behind in the dredger of my incompetence. When I finally finished it I aimed high and faxed it (yes, *faxed* it) to *Climbing* magazine, and the following day I got a fax back saying they loved it. It ended up being included in their book *30 Years of Climbing Magazine* – which was pretty special. Looking back at this first piece, several million words later, I kind of wonder where it all came from.

1.4 Boys Don't Cry

I'd written a few things for *Alpinist* over the years but could see that very often what spoiled this *New Yorker* of the climbing world was the climbing. It just had such a narrow language, of fear, adversity, triumph, personal discovery, all the stuff I'd learnt when I was trying to grasp what writing was. Once you learn the basics of such a narrative you see the cookie-cutter style: start the story at a pivotal moment in the climb, a cliffhanger, then begin at the beginning, introduce everyone, let the hero's journey begin, overcome and triumph – or triumph in not overcoming. Easy. And so once I'd seen this style, I knew I had to try and usurp it, turn it on its head, to write something about climbing that was not about climbing – which is what the best climbing writing is all about.

1.5 Forces

Often the best thing a writer can have is a crash diet of words, to ration them to a point where every single one must count. This piece was written for Patagonia, who I worked for at the time, and rereading it it covers a lot of canvas with only the smallest dab of paint.

1.6 Lessons

This was a blog post and so lacks some of the polish of the other pieces in this section, but then polish is often overrated, and sometimes things are lost in that perfection. This piece was put up on my blog the day we got home, but by then the BBC had seen some of the rushes and freaked out, the fall-out from Jimmy Saville and their duty of care to the young still in the air, and so they asked me to take it down. I think if they could have they'd have binned the film we made, as it was probably more hardcore than anything their adult BBC adventurer types could do, but by then the cat was out the bag, and so it was shown, and was repeated many times. It became a bit of a cult film for kids, and for a few years afterwards mums would come up to me while I was writing and ask, 'Are you Ella's dad?'

1.7 The Troll's Gift

Probably the last great piece of traditional climbing writing I ever did, being over 6,000 words long and taking maybe a few weeks to write, which is unusual for me as I tend to write very quickly. Most of this time was spent going backwards and forwards with Katie Ives, the editor, and it shows. The funny thing about this was all the way through the troll's gift was going to be the gift of failure, but in the last few minutes of writing I realised that the flip side of failure was hope – and that was much more positive. I stopped writing for magazines after this as it seemed to be too much hassle most of the time, and the time spent writing for someone else could be better spent writing for myself.

1.8 Queen Maud Land

I wrote this in an hour on a plane back from Norway, and when I landed my world began to fall apart. This is foreshadowed in this piece, which offers a very rare kind of honesty that's tough to read, but not showy. It's just honest and of that moment.

1.9 Celebrity Abuse

Written as a favour for my mate Ian Parnell, who was the editor of *Climb* magazine, it was different from most things in that it was so throwaway it could be fun as well.

1.10 Edge of Myself

I wrote this the day after climbing the wall, so it was all very fresh in my mind. The funny thing about being so quick to write it all down is that you realise – reading it back – how often it's just as important to let such experiences settle. It was only several months later that I really grasped just how hard that climb was, when I watched some footage from the wall and noticed that my hand was shaking.

1.11 Pizza

I've always been a huge fan of Kurt Vonnegut, and have pretty much lived by his line, 'Peculiar travel suggestions are dancing lessons from God'. This was a nice little jig.

1.12 No Better Knot

I never bought a proper engagement ring, or had a party, so these words were my version of both.

2.13 Imperfect Brother

A piece that shows the power of being your own boss – your own commissioning editor: no one would publish something like this, from a nobody (maybe if I was footballer they would), and yet once published it had a big effect on many people who read it. Out of the blue and often months later people would email me to tell me how much it moved them, and about their own brother or sister, that they recognised themselves in these words and that they had reconnected.

2.14 A Crying Girl

This little thumbnail sketch is typical of my work life, in that I was sitting in my local coffee shop, where I can sit all day, trying to write something else – probably for someone else – when I saw these two. The subtlety of their interaction – the way he sat, the way she leaned – was heartbreaking. Such things go on all around us all the time, but I think most people just keep their eyes forward, their own joy or grief, or the stuff in between – life's filler – enough. I can't help but be a watcher.

2.15 Chongo by the Power

Another one of those pieces of writing that no one would publish, but which many people loved. I'm a bit ambivalent about it, as Chongo is my friend but I feel I'm being cruel to him, abusing him, doing the writer's thing of stealing from someone who's opened themselves up to me. If anything, this is about the cruel writer's eye, which lingers a little longer than most people's, and so sees the crack in the smile.

2.16 Long Runs the Fox

Sometimes, as a writer, you have the ability to give your words as a gift. I could see that maybe Ricky, my friend, was struggling with the choices he'd made, so talented a person yet still cleaning windows. It's not for me to judge if he had done right by his talent, but only to remind him, through my words, that in the eyes of many who had mortgaged their lives that he was our hero for not.

3.17 Life at Retail

Stories are part of human evolution – they have power over how people think, what they do, even what they remember. When you tell stories and you know that just one person reads what you write you have both power and a duty to them. In climbing this means that it's your duty to nudge them into ways of acting that are more responsible, safer – things that will keep them alive and reading on. If you can spin something dry but valuable into a story, and not just a technical description, then it's like a 'dream within a dream', and it can take hold.

3.18 A Mile Further Down the Road

This is the kind of piece that's full of small stories that get tucked into your rucksack, to be taken out when most needed.

4.19. The Haunted Cliff

On the wall I'm as brave a person as you can imagine: daring, dashing, the person I most like to be. But in the real world, like most people, I'm a conformist. I like to think I'm a rebel and a revolutionary, but I now suspect that's how I'm meant to think – a way of thinking that keeps me in line. To be really brave in this twenty-first-century world is to push into uncharted areas of thought and understanding. That's more scary and uncertain and adventurous than any Patagonian spire. This deeper thought about the act of killing babies is just such an adventure.

4.20. A Piece of Wood

A good example of writing about everything and nothing, about loneliness, depression and feeling someone you love slip away. Or a about a lump of wood – or maybe all of the above.

4.21 Until it Hurts No More

This blog was, like a lot of writing, an open letter to someone, someone whom I cared for, someone I fucked around, a good person – maybe the best person I've ever met – who got sucked into the whirlpool of my life. It was written because I could not find the strength to just ring her and say these things – because I'm a coward I guess, who hides behind his fancy words.

As a postscript to this, a few years later I deleted it, the words no longer needed, a dark charm that had used up its small magic. But then people began to ask where it was, telling me that these words had the power to make someone else feel there is an end – and there is. As I write these very words I have my eye on the clock, a date set to meet this very person for a cup of coffee, not to talk about these times, but maybe to demonstrate to each other that it hurts no more.

4.22 The Boat
Almost too raw to reread, but something that has value in its honesty about the realities of human animal relationships.

4.23 Everest Sucking on the Barrel
This is one of those things you write in ten minutes but that hangs around for years. How true is this piss-take of the Everest game? Well, I received many emails from guides who worked those tables who agreed it was true.

4.24 Words like Morphine
In *Ace Ventura: Pet Detective*, Jim Carrey says, 'If I'm not back in five minutes … just wait longer'. I have trouble spelling the word 'suicide', this spelling here taking several attempts, my spellcheck never giving me any useful clues at all. Perhaps it's designed to stymy someone trying to write out their final note to the world – that last kiss or fuck-you. Such notes are intriguing if you're a writer, and great if you're someone who likes the last word. Kenneth Halliwell's suicide note after killing Joe Orton sticks in my mind – nine hammer blows to his lover's head, then a quick note before doing himself to death: *'If you read his diary, all will be explained. KH PS: Especially the latter part.'* If you can't spell, then Google trumps any spellcheck: type in almost anything and it works out what you mean, the mind's arrow equivalent to the spellcheck atomic bomb. When you do google the word the first thing that comes up is the phone number for the Samaritans (116 123), which is clever, and I guess must mean that suicide is something well researched. I've thought about suicide a few times, as I think most must do, like the thought of sucking another man's dick, murdering your own child – role play of the impossible. But suicide (had to

google it again) is not quite the same, because it's something that has shadowed me all my life, from the dead man who hanged himself in the stairwell beside my bedroom, to the people who jumped from the high floors of the flats I grew up in, and then all the rest, that noble death of the brave coward. I often wonder if Cobain made such a thing cool and acceptable, two barrels in the mouth – faith no more. Reading *The Savage God* by Al Alvarez is a tonic for such thoughts, it tells you there is no shame to it, that the sin is a modern invention designed to stop mass suicide as a queue jump into heaven (be cut down by a Roman soldier and you're in). Alvarez's book also tells us something we all know, that suicide is ultimately the failure to simply wait, to stick around, for a day, an hour, just to give life's meaning time to return.

4.25 She Walks Away

I'm really intrigued by how people are perceived, how increasingly others don't give you the benefit of the doubt – one wrong word and you've had it. I find that when you stick around, and don't walk away, everyone you meet has some wisdom to impair. I often ask people what one piece of wisdom they've learnt in their lives. Some people can't think of anything, while others trot out some cliché. The best I ever heard was from a man who'd sold ice cream from a van all his life. When I asked him what this had taught him, he thought for a moment, then said: 'People fucking love ice cream.'

4.26 The Artist

The roll call of the BASE dead could fill half this book. Dean was one of the many for whom you knew it was coming, which sounds harsh, if you live with your head in the sand.

4.27 Rabbit Stories

This is kind of an exercise, creating steps of an idea, building up then down again, each block tied to rabbits. As the story tells, it came about after killing a rabbit in a quarry, that one act pulling together several strings, which is often how a story begins.

4.28 After Her

Very often the art of writing is being able to write about the most mundane of things – doing the washing-up, going for a stroll, swimming in a lake – and then tying something deeper into the tale, to give backbone to something that although weighty could not stand alone.

5.29 Roger Godfrin

The stories in this section of the book are like going to a really horrible and dirty cold gym and really hurting yourself – only a gym built for a writer's brain. They all came about during a period when I wrote almost every day, often about subjects that had nothing to do with climbing, most often about the world I saw around me, and frequently guided what people were talking about where I was writing. Often they had a historical angle (history was one subject I was good at at school), but many of the blog posts made me very uncomfortable, and also quite unpopular. I think I was greatly affected by the idea of not being a slave to popularity (reading *Letters from a Stoic* around this time was from where this idea sprang), and that even if I lost every reader then that would be just the price of being who I am. In the end I got more readers, even if I did lose many who could not understand how someone they liked could not think like them. (The very same people often bemoan our polarised world, as if it is something new, or something bad, when really they're saying 'why can't everyone think like me?') This piece about Roger Godfrin came about after reading *Weapons of Mass Instruction* by John Taylor Gatto, where Gatto mentions the story. I was intrigued and started to dig, probably as I was feeling a little like Godfrin, his story like a reverse Pied Piper of Hamelin, a fairy story that all children should know – but never will. What was funny was I knew about the destruction of Oradour-sur-Glane, had heard the story of the church being blown up, but, like Godfrin, instead of listening to my betters and just believing what I was told, I began to dig and unearthed a much more complex and less binary version, which for me made this story about disobedience and animal instinct special.

5.30 How Does a Clock Tick?

This was written just after the hate mail inserted into the story, brought about by some comment I made online about Steven Seagal.

5.31 Learned Helplessness

I used to tell people when they asked what I did for a job, that I was an assassin. It seemed funny, until one day I told someone stood beside me at a talk I was giving and he said 'me too' – only he was. He told me how he killed people in Afghanistan, probably in Iraq too, and about the red tape you had to go through, thirty hours of observation on the target, the report he had to submit entitled 'Pattern of life'. At the time I found this not shocking or unexpected, but just sort of blatantly going on but unreported. It led me to question what was going on, if the media was free to report on the ongoing wars, if what we thought was truth was simply just propaganda. Where this led was dark. Two years later *The Guardian* began to report on special forces death squads, but by then I had lost faith in anything I read, which can only be a good thing.

5.32 Dog

By now things were a little tricky, and although no longer a slave to being liked, most work had dried up for magazines, businesses, schools etc. as it seemed I'd turned into a nutjob – and I guess I was. One thing that kept me faithful was I had a deep conviction that this road I was on was actually providing the correct data to show where me and my world were heading. I wrote about how Trump would be president, how Brexit would happen, how we were being coerced to stop thinking, or if not that, to just keep quiet. I had that feeling – which I did think could well be madness – that I was the only sane person around, well, me and anyone who did not involve themselves in politics or social media. During this period I had a lot of arguments with people, and found that most of what people would say could be predicted, simply because they said what everyone else did. This led to reading about how animals are trained, and about the Russian use of mine dogs, and how that turned out.

Epilogue: What I've Learned

This was an interview for *Rock and Ice*, and true to form I tried to avoid giving the same old answers you get in these kinds of things. The version here is the complete version I wrote, the one *R&I* used being a lot drier and more of what you'd expect – I've never been a big believer in giving people what they want, even editors!

Bad Poetry

I started dabbling in bad poetry when I started writing *The Bear Pit*, as I'd recognised my style of writing was becoming more and more sparse – the idea being the reader would fill in the rest. I didn't know anything about poetry, even how you use full stops, commas etc., so most of the time I was just dabbling. I only realised there was some small power to it – its effect personal – when I tried reading a poem I'd written about my son Ewen, called 'Poem to a Son'. I only got halfway through it in front of an audience before having to stop, overcome with emotion. It made me think that poetry is best read aloud, not left alone in a book.

ACKNOWLEDGEMENTS

No one ever reads the acknowledgements pages, well, apart from those hoping to get a mention, or those imagining they've been left out. So, here goes.

First of all, I need to thank all the editors I've had over the years, both official and unofficial, paid and paid in kind.

The former includes Bernard Newman at *Climber*, Ian Smith and Geoff Birtles at *High*, Alison Osius at *Rock and Ice*, Gill Kent and Neil Pearsons at *On the Edge*, Ian Parnell at *Climb*, Simon Panton at *Northern Soul*, Tony Whittome at Random House, Katie Ives at *Alpinist*, and Jon Barton, Ed Douglas and John Coefield at Vertebrate, plus many other unsung copy editors, proofreaders and translators (German, Italian, Polish, French, Spanish and even Korean). Oh, and Marni Jackson and the Banff Mountain and Wilderness Writing programme.

The latter includes a long-suffering ex-wife (I've married two teachers, which is a bonus if you need someone to teach you how to write and spell), partners (climbing and bed), and friends and enemies – all of whom gave advice on what was good and what was bad. When you're learning to write it's important to listen to many voices, but as you begin to get a grip you turn down the volume until only the most vocal can be heard. (Also, ignore the five-star reviews, and instead try and shame with future words the one-star reviewers into some small reconsideration of your talent.)

I should also thank my English teacher from high school, Mr Parker, who took the time to translate my illegible scribblings and gave me some small praise. This support came at a crucial time in my life, a little thread to pull at while sitting in remedial English classes, not learning 'joined-up writing' like my classmates, but instead learning to read and write aged twelve – a good indicator that writing often has nothing to do with writing. Never miss the chance to blow on the young sparks of talent.

Technology needs a thank you too, from Word and Pages, to Google docs and search (best spellchecker by far for the misshapen brain), and apps like Grammarly. These things make the impossible possible.

I need to thank my wife Vanessa, who has spent many hours trying to make sense of my words in this book. She thought her name should come first, but I like to defy my editors – a good tip for a healthy relationship too – so it's here instead.

Lastly, I was very lucky to pick a sport that had such a rich history of literature, as important to its tribe as climbing itself, where writing about your holidays can be perceived as having artistic merit!

So, thanks to you all, and if you didn't find your name here, my apologies – but have no doubt it will come to me the morning after this book has gone to print.